Cambridge Certificate of Proficiency in English 2

WITH ANSWERS

D0183678

Examination papers from the University of Cambridge Local Examinations Syndicate

CAMBRIDGE
UNIVERSITY PRESS

PUBLISHED BY THE PRESS SYNDICATE OF THE UNIVERSITY OF CAMBRIDGE
The Pitt Building, Trumpington Street, Cambridge, United Kingdom

CAMBRIDGE UNIVERSITY PRESS
The Edinburgh Building, Cambridge CB2 2RU, UK
40 West 20th Street, New York NY 10011–4211, USA
477 Williamstown Road, Port Melbourne, VIC 3207, Australia
Ruiz de Alarcón, 28014 Madrid, Spain
Dock House, The Waterfront, Cape Town 8001, South Africa

http://www.cambridge.org

First published 2002

Printed in the United Kingdom at the University Press, Cambridge

ISBN 0 521 01168 X Student's Book
ISBN 0 521 75109 8 Student's Book with answers
ISBN 0 521 75104 7 Self-study Pack
ISBN 0 521 75107 1 Teacher's Book
ISBN 0 521 75106 3 Set of 2 Cassettes
ISBN 0 521 75105 5 Set of 2 Audio CDs

Contents

Thanks and acknowledgements

The publishers are grateful to the following for permission to reproduce copyright material. It has not always been possible to identify the sources of all the material used and in such cases the publishers would welcome information from the copyright owners.

The New Internationalist for p. 4: 'The Cost of Cool' by Michael Peel © *The New Internationalist*; *Independent* for p. 5: extracted from an article by Sally Staples, first published in *Independent* 14 February 1998; Prospect Publishing Ltd for p. 6: extract from 'Get out of the Kitchen' by Will Skidelsky, originally published in *Prospect* magazine; Gillon Aitken Associates for p. 7: extract from *Risk* by A Alvarez © 1991 by A Alvarez; HarperCollins Publishers for p. 8: extract from *The Blessings of a Good Thick Skirt* by Mary Russell. Also for p. 30: extract from pp. 111–12 from *Notes from a Small Island* by Bill Bryson, Copyright © 1995 by Bill Bryson; Curtis Brown Group Ltd for p. 8: extract from *The Blessings of a Good Thick Skirt* by Mary Russell, reproduced with permission of Curtis Brown Group Ltd, London on behalf of Mary Russell, © Mary Russell 1986; The Peters Fraser and Dunlop Group for p. 9: reproduced from *Funny Water* by Frank Kermode (Copyright © Frank Kermode 2000) in the *London Review of Books* by permission of PFD on behalf of Professor Sir Frank Kermode. Also for p. 12: extract reproduced from *The Uses of Error* by Frank Kermode (Copyright © Frank Kermode 1990) by permission of PFD on behalf of Professor Sir Frank Kermode. Also for pp. 92–93: extract from *Brilliant Creatures* by Clive James, 1984, reprinted by permission of PFD on behalf of Clive James; Blackwell Publishers for pp. 10–11: extract from 'Rethinking work' by Theodore Zeldin © The Chancellor, Masters and Scholars of Oxford University; Penguin Putnam Inc. for p. 16: extract from DREAM POWER by Ann Faraday. Used by permission of Coward-McCann, Inc., a division of Penguin Putnam Inc.; The Random House Group and The Peters Fraser and Dunlop Group for p. 22: extract from ALL TOGETHER NOW by John Harvey Jones published by Heinemann. Used by permission of the Random House Group Limited. PFD on behalf of Sir John Harvey Jones; A. P. Watt Ltd for p. 23: extract from *The Way to Win* by Will Carling and Robert Heller, by permission of A. P. Watt Ltd on behalf of Heller Arts Ltd and Will Carling. Also for pp. 84–85: extract from *The Razor's Edge* by W Somerset Maugham, reproduced by permission of A. P. Watt Ltd on behalf of the Royal Literary Fund; Transworld Publishers for p. 30 © Bill Bryson. Extracted from NOTES FROM A SMALL ISLAND, published by Transworld Publisher, a division of the Random House Group Ltd. All rights reserved; *Scientific American* for p. 32: adapted from 'Divided We Fall; Cooperation among Lions' by Craig Packer and Anne E. Pussey. Copyright © May 1997 by Scientific American, Inc. All rights reserved; Charlotte Raven for p. 31: extract from 'It does what it says on the label' in *The Guardian* 16/05/2000; *The Sunday Times* for p. 33: extract from 'Crucial Cuts: Blur, Parklife' by Robert Sandall; Hodder and Stoughton Educational for p. 35: extract from *Teach Yourself Writing a Novel and Getting Published* by Nigel Watts, reproduced by permission of Hodder and Stoughton Educational Limited; *The Guardian* for pp. 36–37: extract from 'Are we getting enough?' by Andy Beckett © *The Guardian* 16/05/2000; Arnold for pp. 38–39: extract from *Television, Broadcasting, Flow: Key Metaphors in TV Theory* (Gripsrud) by Christine Geraghty &

David Lusted (Eds); Philip Allan Updates for p. 51: extract from 'The Right to Roam' by Susan Care in *Psychology Review*, February 2000; Telegraph Group Limited for pp. 58–59: extract from 'The Best Port in a Storm' by Jo Knowsley © Telegraph Group Limited 2000. Also for p. 105: extract from 'Comfort in the Obsolete' by Wendy Grossman © Telegraph Group Limited 2000; *Archaeology Today* for p. 59: extract from 'Artificial Anasazi' by George J. Gumerman & Jeffrey S. Dean; The Women's Press for p. 60: extract from *Taking Reality by Surprise* by Susan Sellers, published in Great Britain by The Women's Press Ltd, 1991, 34 Great Sutton Street, London EC1V 0LQ; A & C Black for p. 61: extract from *Writing Popular Fiction* by Rona Randall, 1997; F & W Publications Inc. for p. 62: excerpted from *The Insider's Guide to Writing for Screen and Television*, Copyright © 1997 by Ronald Tobias. Used with permission of Writer's Digest Books, an imprint of F & W Publications, Inc. All rights reserved; *The Geographical Magazine* for pp. 64–65: extract from 'The Heat is On' by Nick Middleton, extracted from *Geographical* Vol. 72 No. 1, www.geographical.co.uk; ITPS Ltd for p. 66: extract from *Maps and Their Makers* by G R Crone; Oxford University Press for p. 71: extract from *Social and Cultural Anthropology* by John Monaghan and Peter Just © John Monaghan and Peter Just 2000, by permission of Oxford University Press; Oneworld Publications for p. 77: extract from *The Fifth Dimension* © John Hick, 1999. Reproduced by permission of Oneworld Publications; Pearson Education Limited for p. 86: extract from *The Pursuit of History* by John Tosh; Cambridge University Press for p. 87: extract from *An Introduction to Animal Behaviour* by Aubrey Manning and Marian Stamp Dawkins, 1992; Nelson Thornes Ltd for p. 88: extract from *Fundamentals of Sociology* by McNeill & Townley; The Associated Board of the Royal Schools of Music for pp. 90–91: extract from 'The Challenge Ahead' by Dr Susan Hallam. This article first appeared in *Libretto*, the journal of The Associated Board of the Royal Schools of Music. The Economist for p. 104: extract from 'The end of work?' © *The Economist* Newspaper Limited, London, 28 September 1996.

Colour section photographs:
Allsport/Julian Herbert: 4D; AP Photos/Lennox McLendon: 3F; Pacific Stock/Bruce Coleman Collection: 4B; Corbis Stock Market: 3E; Michael Marchant/Environmental Images: 2A, Steve Morgan/Environmental Images: 2B and 2D, Trevor Perry/Environmental Images: 2F, Martin Bond/Environmental Images: 2G; Getty Images/Stephen Derr: 1B, Getty Images/Michael Rosenfeld: 1D, Getty Images/V.C.L: 1E and 1F, Getty Images/ Paul Chesley: 1G, Getty Images/Ed Pritchard: 2C, Getty Images/ Adri Berger: 3B, Getty Images/Dennis Kitchen: 3C, Getty Images/Masterfile: 3D, Getty Images/Martine Mouchy: 4A, Getty Images/Pal Hermansen: 4C; PA Photos/EPA: 1A, PA Photos/Toby Melville: 1C, PA Photos/David Jones: 4E; Courtesy Planet Organic: 2E; The Photographers Library: 3A.

Picture research by Sandie Huskinson-Rolfe of PHOTOSEEKERS

Cover design by Dunne & Scully

The cassettes and audio CDs which accompany this book were recorded at Studio AVP, London

To *the student*

This book is for candidates preparing for the University of Cambridge Local Examinations Syndicate (UCLES) Certificate of Proficiency in English (CPE) examination. It contains four complete tests which reflect the most recent CPE specifications (introduced in December 2002).

The CPE is part of a group of examinations developed by UCLES called the Cambridge Main Suite. The Main Suite consists of five examinations which have similar characteristics but which are designed for different levels of English ability. Within the five levels, CPE is at Cambridge Level 5.

Cambridge Level 5 Certificate of Proficiency in English (CPE)
Cambridge Level 4 Certificate in Advanced English (CAE)
Cambridge Level 3 First Certificate in English (FCE)
Cambridge Level 2 Preliminary English Test (PET)
Cambridge Level 1 Key English Test (KET)

The CPE examination consists of five papers:

Paper 1	**Reading**	1 hour 30 minutes
Paper 2	**Writing**	2 hours
Paper 3	**Use of English**	1 hour 30 minutes
Paper 4	**Listening**	40 minutes (approximately)
Paper 5	**Speaking**	19 minutes

Paper 1   Reading
This paper consists of four parts with 40 questions, which take the form of three multiple-choice tasks and a gapped text task. Part 1 contains three short texts, Part 2 contains four short texts and Parts 3 and 4 each contain one longer text. The texts are taken from fiction, non-fiction, journals, magazines, newspapers, and promotional and informational materials. This paper is designed to test candidates' ability to understand the meaning of written English at word, phrase, sentence, paragraph and whole text level.

Paper 2   Writing
This paper consists of two writing tasks in a range of formats (e.g. letter, report, review, article, essay, proposal). Candidates are asked to complete two tasks, writing between 300 and 350 words for each. Part 1 (Question 1) consists of one compulsory task based on instructions and a short text. Part 2 (Questions 2–5) consists of one task which candidates select from a choice of four. Question 5 has a task on one of each of three set texts. Assessment is based on achievement of task, range and accuracy of vocabulary and grammatical structures, organisation, content and appropriacy of register and format.

Paper 3   Use of English
This paper consists of five parts with 44 questions. These take the form of an open cloze, a word formation task, gapped sentences, key word transformations and two texts with comprehension questions and a summary writing task. The paper is designed to assess candidates' ability to demonstrate knowledge and control of the language system by completing these tasks which are at text and sentence level.

Paper 4   Listening
This paper consists of four parts with 28 questions, which take the form of two multiple-choice tasks, a sentence-completion task and a three-way matching task. Part 1 contains four short extracts and Parts 2 to 4 each contain one longer text. The texts are audio-recordings based on a variety of sources including interviews, discussions, lectures, conversations and documentary features. The paper is designed to assess candidates' ability to understand the meaning of spoken English, to extract information from a spoken text and to understand speakers' attitudes and opinions.

Paper 5   Speaking
The Speaking Test consists of three parts, which take the form of an interview section, a collaborative task and individual long turns with follow-up discussion. The test is designed to elicit a wide range of language from both candidates. Candidates are examined in pairs by two examiners, an Interlocutor and an Assessor. The Assessor awards a mark based on the following criteria: Grammatical Resource, Lexical Resource, Discourse Management, Pronunciation and Interactive Communication. The Interlocutor provides a global mark for the whole test.

Marks and results

The five CPE papers total 200 marks, after weighting. Each paper is weighted to 40 marks.

A candidate's overall CPE grade is based on the total score gained in all five papers. It is not necessary to achieve a satisfactory level in all five papers in order to pass the examination. Pass grades are A, B or C, with A being the highest. D and E are failing grades. The minimum successful performance in order to achieve Grade C corresponds to about 60% of the total marks. Every candidate is provided with a Statement of Results which includes a graphical display of their performance in each paper. These are shown against the scale Exceptional – Good – Borderline – Weak and indicate the candidate's relative performance in each paper.

The CPE examination is recognised by the majority of British universities for English language entrance requirements.

Further information

For more information about CPE or any other UCLES examination contact:

EFL Information
University of Cambridge Local Examinations Syndicate
1 Hills Road
Cambridge
CB1 2EU
United Kingdom

Tel: +44 1223 553355
Fax: +44 1223 460278
e-mail: efl@ucles.org.uk
http://www.cambridge-efl.org.uk

In some areas, this information can also be obtained from the British Council.

Test 1

PAPER 1   READING (1 hour 30 minutes)

Part 1

For questions **1–18**, read the three texts below and decide which answer (**A**, **B**, **C** or **D**) best fits each gap.

Mark your answers **on the separate answer sheet**.

Air-conditioning

There is a chill in the air at Cannons Gym, a favourite lunch-time haunt for City of London workers. To deal with this summer's unusually high temperatures, the fitness centre has gone **(1)** .... with the air-conditioning. **(2)** .... , in fact, that at quiet times, the gym feels like somewhere in the Arctic. This is just one example of how the modern world casually **(3)** .... air-conditioning. It has become a central feature of work and play, a potent **(4)** .... of the ability of humanity to control the climate, or at least modify it.

Many air-conditioned buildings, however, could **(5)** .... other methods of cooling. They could take advantage of daylight and natural ventilation and have thicker walls that absorb less heat during the day and radiate it away at night. These **(6)** .... may sound obvious, but they can have telling results and would considerably reduce the need for air-conditioning.

1 A	overweight	**B**	overboard	**C**	overtime	**D**	overblown
2 A	So much so	**B**	So as to	**C**	So to speak	**D**	So be it
3 A	malfunctions	**B**	outdoes	**C**	superimposes	**D**	misuses
4 A	symbol	**B**	token	**C**	emblem	**D**	label
5 A	empower	**B**	engage	**C**	employ	**D**	enlist
6 A	outcomes	**B**	measures	**C**	resolutions	**D**	actions

Sundials

It is surely more than coincidence that the beginning of a new millennium is being **(7)** .... by renewed interest in sundials: instruments used to measure time according to the position of the sun. A hundred years ago, they were a vital time-keeping **(8)** .... , essential for anyone who hoped to keep

4

their clocks working accurately. Then, as clocks and watches became more sophisticated and reliable, the sundial was relegated to the **(9)** .... of garden ornament – a romantic and intriguing ornament, but **(10)** .... an anachronism, in a brave new technological age. Now the clock has been turned back and they are again being taken seriously.

David Harber, a sundial maker, believes that their appeal **(11)** .... in their direct link with the planets. He says that when he delivers one, there is a **(12)** .... of magic when it starts working. They are still, calm, romantic objects that remind us of our place in the cosmos.

7	**A**	associated	**B**	accompanied	**C**	acquainted	**D**	aroused
8	**A**	device	**B**	utensil	**C**	piece	**D**	item
9	**A**	cluster	**B**	set	**C**	group	**D**	status
10	**A**	conversely	**B**	after all	**C**	nonetheless	**D**	in turn
11	**A**	stands	**B**	displays	**C**	evolves	**D**	lies
12	**A**	moment	**B**	point	**C**	time	**D**	pause

Paint Your Own China

My image of china-painting **(13)** .... from a visit, long ago, to an arts and crafts exhibition where stern-looking grey-haired ladies demonstrated how to cover a teacup with delicate flowers using a **(14)** .... of deft brushstrokes. The spectacle was **(15)** .... , because each stroke formed a perfect petal or leaf. Their hands never wobbled, the paint never smudged, and the observer might have concluded that these women had either been **(16)** .... their art for decades or had been born with an extraordinary talent for steady precision.

(17) .... of this experience, I wondered what kind of people would have the courage to enrol on a course in china-painting. Would even the beginners display an **(18)** .... artistry? In fact, the atmosphere turned out to be far from intimidating. The students were all there to have fun and not even the tutor wanted to paint petals on teacups with the robotic rapidity I had remembered.

13	**A**	stemmed	**B**	initiated	**C**	commenced	**D**	instigated
14	**A**	string	**B**	collection	**C**	series	**D**	procession
15	**A**	sensitive	**B**	riveting	**C**	charismatic	**D**	distinctive
16	**A**	practising	**B**	exercising	**C**	working	**D**	expressing
17	**A**	In respect	**B**	Careful	**C**	On reflection	**D**	Mindful
18	**A**	intuitive	**B**	inward	**C**	inverted	**D**	integral

Part 2

You are going to read four extracts which are all concerned in some way with activities. For questions **19–26**, choose the answer (**A**, **B**, **C** or **D**) which you think fits best according to the text.

Mark your answers **on the separate answer sheet**.

The Lure of the Kitchen

When I was at university I decided I wanted to be a chef. Among my contemporaries, this was an unusual choice. Cooking was not one of the plum jobs that most of us wanted. It is, on the face of it, an unattractive profession. Chefs lead notoriously harsh lives: the work is long, pressured, menial – and badly paid.

But such considerations didn't put me off. I was unhappy at university. The work was hard; the social scene was insular and self-important. Being a chef seemed the perfect antidote to intellectual and social posturing. It promised a seriousness and integrity lacking in my college life.

But my desire to cook was not simply a reaction to being a student. It also expressed an aesthetic ideal. My first glimpse of this ideal came when I ate a meal at a famous London restaurant. It was a revelation. I still clearly remember my starter. I finished that meal wanting to prostrate myself, weeping, at the feet of the chef who had made it. I felt warm and airy for days afterwards.

After this, I developed an intense desire to uncover the secrets of this strange, fabulous art. I transformed my student life into an extended preparation for my assault on the culinary world. My history degree became a hollow pretence, distracting me from my true course. I acquired my real education haphazardly and deficiently by reading cookbooks, roaming markets and delicatessens and preparing extravagant meals.

19 What attracted the writer to the idea of becoming a chef?

   A   He wanted to express his creativity.
   B   The work involved seemed real and worthwhile.
   C   He wanted to stand out from the crowd.
   D   His fellow students were unconvinced by the idea.

20 How did the writer pursue his study of cookery?

   A   reluctantly
   B   aggressively
   C   fervently
   D   systematically

Extract from a novel

The school's swimming instructor was an ex-drill sergeant, small and muscle-bound, with tattooed arms. When I asked him to teach me how to dive, he told me to sit on the pool's edge, put my hands above my head and roll forwards, pushing myself off with my feet. I practised that manoeuvre until the hour was up. The next visit, he got me standing upright, and diving off the edge. The instructor was a martinet and every time I surfaced he looked at me with distaste: 'Don't look down, look up!' 'Keep your legs straight.' 'Point your toes I said!' The next week, I went up onto the high board. It was a fixed board and its front edge bent slightly downward. It seemed outrageously high as I stood there, trying to work up my courage. Gradually the echoing voices disappeared and I felt as if I were cocooned in silence. I waved my arms vaguely in the way I'd been   **line 11**
taught, tried to look up, not down, and launched myself into space. For a brief   **line 12**
moment, I was flying. When I hit the water, I crumpled ignominiously, and my   **line 13**
legs were all over the place. The instructor looked at me with contempt and
shook his head. But even he could not diminish my euphoria. That's what they   **line 15**
mean by 'free as a bird', I thought.

21   The writer remembers his instructor as someone

    A   who resented him.
    B   who inhibited him.
    C   who despised his technique.
    D   whom he wanted to impress.

22   Which phrase explains the writer's feeling of euphoria (line 15)?

    A   'cocooned in silence' (line 11)
    B   'I crumpled ignominiously' (line 13)
    C   'launched myself into space' (line 12)
    D   'I was flying' (line 13)

THE TRAVELLER

To those of us for whom a comfortable bed, running water and the probability of living at least until tomorrow are of prime importance, the phenomenon of the traveller appears as incomprehensible as it is intriguing. Here are people who have succumbed to the treacherous seduction of the unknown, who actually choose to put their lives at risk by climbing the sheer and icy face of an avalanche-ridden mountain; who sail alone in frail craft through towering seas; who will eat maggots and river insects if nothing more palatable is on offer and who can live, day and night for months on end, in the shadow and the promise of the unknown.

It is easy to dismiss such people as oddities – as indeed they are – to be relegated to the ranks of the truly eccentric: hermits, freefall divers or indeed writers. That they exist cannot be denied, but the strange, uncomfortable world they occupy lies well outside our everyday experience and can be dismissed, we tell ourselves, as an irrelevancy. We can shrug our shoulders and return thankfully to our world of microwave ovens and answerphones, glad that the only risks to our own health are predictable ones such as making a suicidal dash across a city street.

23 According to the writer, what motivates travellers?

A a desire for a solitary existence
B a dissatisfaction with modern living
C a need to discover new things
D a fascination with outdoor life

24 The writer emphasises the contrast between his world and that of the traveller by

A likening travellers to freefall divers.
B illustrating his indifference to travellers.
C mentioning the dangers of city living.
D referring to domestic appliances.

SAILING

Jonathan Raban is afraid of the sea, saying it is not his element, which is probably why he spends so much time on it. He does not claim to be a world-class sailor, though he is obviously a competent one. His overriding reason for sailing is that, being a writer, he likes to write about having sailed. Sailing is guaranteed to provide alarms and achievements for his pen to celebrate.

Raban's little boat carries an electronic device that instantly gives mariners their position to within a few metres, anywhere on the earth's surface. Strongly as he approves of this instrument, there is more than a touch of primitivism in Raban's attitude to other sea-faring aids. He thinks the invention of the compass was a disaster, causing a 'fundamental rift in the relationship between man and sea'. Raban maintains that since it came into use, perhaps a thousand years ago, it has become the main object of the steersman's gaze, with the result that he no longer has to study the waves and *feel* the sea. And the ocean, once a *place* with all sorts of things going on in it, is now reduced to a mere space. Since his job is merely to keep steady on a course, the helmsman can be replaced for long stretches by an autopilot. This may be why Raban had time to look so carefully at the waves.

25 What is Jonathan Raban's main motivation for sailing?

    A   He needs to conquer his fear of the sea.
    B   He wants to gain recognition as a sailor.
    C   It offers him experiences he can use afterwards.
    D   It provides a contrast to his existence on land.

26 What is the writer doing when he talks about the compass in paragraph 2?

    A   illustrating Raban's skills
    B   questioning Raban's attitude
    C   defending Raban's assumptions
    D   supporting Raban's view

Part 3

You are going to read an extract from an article. Seven paragraphs have been removed from the extract. Choose from the paragraphs **A–H** the one which fits each gap (**27–33**). There is one extra paragraph which you do not need to use.

Mark your answers **on the separate answer sheet**.

Work

Theodore Zeldin looks at how our working life could change.

Are you as respected and appreciated as you deserve? Success in a career is no longer enough. Every profession is complaining that it is not properly valued or understood, and even among individuals who have won eminence, there is often bitterness behind the fame. Loving your work, until recently, was enough to make you a member of an envied minority. But now you have to ask yourself what your job is doing to you as a person, to your mind, character and relationships.

27	

To counter this, I am trying to discover how work could have the fulfilment of these aspirations as its first priority – instead of treating us as clay to be moulded to suit industrial purposes – and how it could be reconceived to suit us all, both women and men. It would have to be not just a way of creating wealth, but a worthwhile style of life, a path to a fuller existence, to the discovery of unsuspected talents and to a wider variety of human contacts.

28	

Even the middle-class professions, however, no longer have the liberating appeal they once had. Doctors are often more stressed than their patients and complain about the failure of clinical medicine. Accountants, despite unprecedented influence, are troubled by doubts about their profession's ethics. Most architects never get the chance to exercise their imaginations freely. Administrators are paralysed by their own bureaucracy. The middle managers, who once gloried in their status, are, as a European study reveals, losing their conviction.

29	

I have embarked on an investigation of a wide range of occupations, one by one, to see how each shapes and sometimes destroys those in it. I have studied how the notion of what humans are capable of has been expanded in different civilisations, and how courage can be manufactured. I have applied my method to the major preoccupations of our time – happiness, love, friendship and respect.

30	

How many of us can say that we are fully alive at work? How many of us are really part-time slaves – theoretically having the right to escape from our drudgery, but in reality virtual prisoners of our qualifications and careers, used as instruments by others, working not so that we might become better people, but because we can see no other option? Take hotel workers as an example, since 10 per cent of the working population is now in the 'hospitality industry'. The amount of unused potential is unbelievable. Many highly intelligent and lively people put up with low prestige, low salaries and long hours.

31	

A large proportion of hotel staff are foreigners too, keen to learn a new language and discover a new civilisation, but they have the most superficial relations with their guests. Hotels could be cultural centres, active intermediaries between the guest and the city, genuine hosts bringing together people who have not met. Hoteliers could use the knowledge of the many students they employ, instead of giving them only menial tasks.

32	

The time has come to rethink what this term denotes – from a human, not just a financial angle – and to move on from traditional categorisations. For me, work is a relationship. Now that many people are not content with relations based on obedience, and regard work as an assertion of independence or temperament, they must be given a chance to design their own jobs, and choose their own colleagues, even their customers, within the limits of practicality and profitability.

33	

This is a more intimate encounter, which creates a bond of respect between the participants, and is valued as a way of getting inside another person's skin, with the likelihood that one will be changed by the experience. It is more than a relaxation, because it is the most effective means of establishing equality. Every time you have a conversation which achieves that, the world is changed by a minute amount.

A This means that they have to know how to converse across the boundaries of professional jargon, with minds that may at first seem quite alien. Everybody is clear about the importance of communication, but it is a very different thing from conversation, and traditional conversation is very different from the new kind of conversation which people feel the lack of today.

B However, this remodelling would not mean abolishing unemployment. This is too simple a goal, because the more people are educated, the more they demand jobs that are life-enhancing, interesting and useful. A lifetime of work has to be seen as a work of art, with the fulfilled individual at its centre.

C If they paid closer attention to their staff's deepest ambitions, they would realise that there were many other services that hotels could provide. But they are restrained by the accountants, who say that firms, in order to maximise their profits, should concentrate on one core activity.

D This is because there has been no serious rethinking of what a hotel is since the days of the Ritz, with its nineteenth-century idea of luxury. A hotel is not just a place where travellers sleep, but a United Nations in miniature. People from all over the world meet at hotels, though they usually pass each other in silence.

E Having looked at those areas, I am now focusing on the search for more satisfying ways of earning a living. There is no shortage of experts devoting themselves to prolonging the life and increasing the income of corporations and institutions. But auditing our finances is not enough: we need to make an audit of ourselves as human beings too, and discover with what sort of people we want to spend our lives.

F Meanwhile, the business corporations and public institutions in which these people work are slimming. The panaceas of decentralised decision-making, increasing skills and performance-related rewards have not succeeded in winning commitment from employees. In Britain, only 8 per cent of employees 'are strongly of the view that their values and those of their organisations are very similar'.

G This question is crucial. For however brilliant your skills, if they make you a bore, unable to converse with those outside your speciality, if you are so busy with detail that you have no time to acquire wisdom or exercise your imagination or humour, then no amount of status or financial reward will compensate for your inadequacy as a human being.

H Hotels know so little about their guests – and often about their staff – even though they spend vast sums on sophisticated IT systems to store the rather unsophisticated data they collect. Managers cling to notions of customer service based on far too simple a view of what produces 'guest satisfaction'.

Part 4

You are going to read an introduction from a book of essays. For questions **34–40**, choose the answer (**A**, **B**, **C** or **D**) which you think fits best according to the text.

Mark your answers **on the separate answer sheet**.

Writing Reviews

Frank Kermode examines the craft of review-writing from a practitioner's point of view.

Most reviews are written and circulated under conditions which ensure that they have a very short active life. There are deadlines, there are restrictions, normally quite severe, on their length; and when published they claim houseroom only for as long as the newspaper they are printed in – a day or a week, at most a month. Moreover, the literary status of reviews tends to be settled by their ephemerality. It is usually supposed, not only by the public but, quite often, by the writers themselves, that reviewing is work that nobody would do if there weren't some reason – shortage of cash would be cited most often, though another good reason is that you can't work all day on a novel or a 'serious' book of any sort – which prevents them from occupying their time with something more valuable.

Yet reviewing is a skilled and multi-faceted job. It is one thing to be bright, brisk and summarily fair in the six or eight hundred words of an ordinary newspaper review, quite another to control, without looseness of argument, the six or eight thousand words sometimes allowed by international journals. And the fifteen hundred words of a leading piece in the weekly magazines present some of the problems of both short and long. Not that length is the only consideration. For one thing, the reviewer obviously needs to think about the probable audience, the weekend skimmer at one end of the scale, the person already inter- ested enough in the subject to tackle a serious review- article at the other. Finally, a reviewer needs to know quite a bit about quite a number of things; and must be able to write prose that intelligent people can understand and enjoy. It follows almost infallibly that the reviewer will be somebody who writes other things besides reviews.

The American novelist John Updike, who rather looks down on criticism – 'hugging the shore' he calls it – nevertheless enjoys some coastal reviewing in the intervals between his transoceanic novel-writing. Understandably reluctant to allow even his less ambitious voyages to go without any permanent record, he gathers together his every review, however short, into volumes with mildly self-deprecating titles. It might be thought that lesser persons should accept ephemerality as the penalty appropriate to their coastal caution; but it is hard to see why, if they can get away with it, they shouldn't be allowed to enjoy the measure of permanence, and the measure of vanity, proper to their station, especially if they believe that some of their best writing has been 'buried' in reviews. I admit to feeling this about my own work.

My own principal occupation has been academic, and most of my 'serious' books are recognisably academic products, the sort of thing professors like, and are expected to do as part of their jobs. However, the English-speaking world (I think fortunately) acknowledges nothing comparable to the sharp distinction people from other cultures make between reviewing and literary study – and so with us it is quite usual for the same people to do both. The days are gone when other academics reviled reviewer-professors for unseemly self-display, or waste of academic time, or betrayal of the dignity of their institutions. And complaints from non- professors, to the effect that the professors are taking the bread out of their mouths, are also less common than they were, partly because there is so much more reviewing nowadays that practically everyone can have some, partly, no doubt, because the bread is often such a meagre ration.

My own view is that these arrangements are good for both readers – since they can be fairly certain the reviewer has at least some idea what he is talking about – and professors, if only because the work helps to keep them sane. It also reminds them that they have a duty, easily neglected, to make themselves intelligible to non-professors. When talking among themselves they may feel some need to be impressively arcane, but when addressing intelligent non- professors they need to make sure they are communicating effectively.

Finally, it is clear that for a variety of reasons, and despite all that can be said to dignify it, reviewing must normally be a secondary occupation. It is something you can only do well enough if you are also doing something else well enough.

34 What does the writer say about reviews in the first paragraph?

  A Their topicality means that they are eagerly read.
  B They may be considered an inferior form of writing.
  C The best reviews tend to be written by novelists.
  D They provide writers with a regular income.

35 The writer says that a good reviewer is someone who

  A bears in mind the different types of reader.
  B has in-depth knowledge of the topic.
  C concentrates on reviewing as a career.
  D adopts a clearly defined style.

36 How does John Updike appear to regard review-writing?

  A He thinks it may help a writer to widen his readership.
  B He is unwilling to write any reviews himself.
  C He supports a writer's right to criticise the work of others.
  D He considers it an unchallenging, unimaginative type of writing.

37 How does the writer feel about the less well-known writers who publish their reviews in book form?

  A They should leave reviewing to the great writers.
  B Their best work is to be found in their reviews.
  C They are entitled to some pride in their work.
  D They do not deserve long-term success.

38 How have attitudes changed towards academics who write reviews?

  A Non-academics have agreed to share out reviewing work available.
  B Their colleagues have come to regard it as an acceptable activity.
  C Less resentment exists now that reviewing can provide a reasonable income.
  D Greater understanding results from academic standards being less rigorously applied.

39 Why is the writer in favour of academics also working on reviews?

  A The general reader is able to rely on their knowledge.
  B Review-writing is the most enjoyable part of a professor's work.
  C Feedback gained from non-academics is useful for their research.
  D Their level of language is appropriate for review-writing.

40 In writing this text, the writer's main intention is to

  A justify the academic status of reviews.
  B defend a particular reviewer.
  C improve the perception of review-writing.
  D encourage other authors to take up review-writing.

PAPER 2   WRITING (2 hours)

Part 1

You **must** answer this question. Write your answer in **300–350** words in an appropriate style.

---

1   A magazine is inviting readers to send in articles on whether life in the countryside is preferable to life in the city. You read the personal account below and decide to write an article called 'Escape to the country – should you?', responding to the points raised and expressing your own opinions.

> 'When we left the city I was stressed by the pace of life and travelling to work, and had little time with my children. I was sure the cleaner air and green spaces would be good for us. At first it seemed the right move. There was no commuting, noise or dirt, and our money went further. But then I discovered that life in the country also had drawbacks...'

Write your **article**.

Part 2

Write an answer to **one** of the questions **2–5** in this part. Write your answer in **300–350** words in an appropriate style.

2 A company wants to launch a new soft drink onto the market, and is running a competition inviting people to send in proposals for different ways of advertising it. The company wants people to comment on the use of the media, famous personalities, free gifts, and other advertising techniques, and explain why they think their ideas will be particularly effective. You decide to send in a proposal.

Write your **proposal**.

3 You are a member of your school/college theatre group which has recently performed a play with great success at an International Festival of Drama. The editor of your school/college magazine has asked you to write a review of the International Festival of Drama and say what you learned from the experience.

Write your **review**.

4 Your college is producing a handbook to make new students from abroad feel welcome. The editor has asked you to write a letter for inclusion. The letter should explain how to make the best use of college facilities (e.g. canteen, library, IT suite, sports hall) and give information and advice on clubs, societies and student services.

Write your **letter**. Do not write any postal addresses.

5 Based on your reading of **one** of these books, write on **one** of the following.

(a) Anne Tyler: *The Accidental Tourist*
You see the following comment in a student magazine: 'There are few books which manage to be both funny and sad.' You write a review in which you discuss this comment in relation to *The Accidental Tourist*.

Write your **review**.

(b) John Wyndham: *The Day of the Triffids*
During a class discussion of *The Day of the Triffids*, your tutor quotes from the book:
'There is more to the Triffids than we think'. Your tutor asks you to write an essay in which you briefly describe the triffids, and outline their role in the novel, discussing their impact on the society in the novel.

Write your **essay**.

(c) Graham Greene: *Our Man in Havana*
A literary journal has published an article which argues that there were no heroes in twentieth-century English literature. You write a letter to the editor in which you respond to this statement, referring to Graham Greene's portrayal of Wormold in *Our Man in Havana*, stating whether or not you think he achieves the status of a hero.

Write your **letter**. Do not write any postal addresses.

PAPER 3   USE OF ENGLISH (1 hour 30 minutes)

Part 1

For questions **1–15**, read the text below and think of the word which best fits each space. Use only **one** word in each space. There is an example at the beginning **(0)**.

Write your answers in CAPITAL LETTERS **on the separate answer sheet**.

Example: | 0 | H | A | V | E | | | | | | | | | | | | | | | | |

Dreams

Dreams **(0)** ..*have*.... always fascinated human beings. The idea that dreams provide us with useful information about our lives goes **(1)** .... thousands of years. For the greater **(2)** .... of human history **(3)** .... was taken for granted that the sleeping mind was in touch with the supernatural world and dreams were to be interpreted as messages with prophetic or healing functions. In the nineteenth century, **(4)** .... was a widespread reaction **(5)** .... this way of thinking and dreams were widely dismissed as being very **(6)** .... more than jumbles of fantasy **(7)** .... about by memories of the previous day.

It was not **(8)** .... the end of the nineteenth century **(9)** .... an Austrian neurologist, Sigmund Freud, pointed out that people who have similar experiences during the day, and who are then subjected **(10)** .... the same stimuli when they are asleep, produce different dreams. Freud **(11)** .... on to develop a theory of the dream process which **(12)** .... enable him to interpret dreams as clues to the conflicts taking place within the personality. It is by no **(13)** .... an exaggeration to say that **(14)** .... any other theories have had **(15)** .... great an influence on subsequent thought.

Part 2

For questions **16–25**, read the text below. Use the word given in capitals at the end of some of the lines to form a word that fits in the space in the same line. There is an example at the beginning **(0)**.

Write your answers in CAPITAL LETTERS **on the separate answer sheet**.

Example: | **0** | E | C | O | N | O | M | I | C | | | | | | | | | | | | |

Food miles

In Britain, what is described as 'food miles', the distance which food is transported from the place where it is grown to its point of sale, continues to rise. This has major **(0)** ..economic.., social and environmental consequences,   **ECONOMY**
given the traffic congestion and pollution which **(16)** .... follow.   **VARIABLE**

According to **(17)** .... groups, the same amount of food is travelling   **PRESS**
50 per cent further than twenty years ago. What's more, the rise in the
demand for road haulage over this period has mostly been due to the transport of food and drink. The groups assert that the increase in the number
of lorry journeys is **(18)** .... and that many of these are far from   **EXCEED**
(19) ....   **ESSENCE**

In the distribution systems employed by British food **(20)** .... , fleets of   **RETAIL**
lorries bring all goods into more **(21)** .... located warehouses for   **CENTRE**
redistribution across the country. **(22)** .... as this might appear, the   **LOGIC**
situation whereby some goods get sent back to the same areas from which
they came is **(23)** ....   **AVOID**

In response to scathing **(24)** .... from environmentalists, some food   **CRITIC**
distributors now aim to minimise the impact of food miles by routing vehicles,
wherever possible, on motorways after dark. This encourages greater energy
(25) .... whilst also reducing the impact on the residential areas through   **EFFICIENT**
which they would otherwise pass.

Part 3

For questions **26–31**, think of **one** word only which can be used appropriately in all three sentences. Here is an example **(0)**.

Example:

0 Some of the tourists are hoping to get compensation for the poor state of the hotel, and I think they have a very .... case.

There's no point in trying to wade across the river, the current is far too ....

If you're asking me which of the candidates should get the job, I'm afraid I don't have any .... views either way.

Write **only** the missing word in CAPITAL LETTERS **on the separate answer sheet**.

---

26 If it's only a .... of a few pence, it hardly seems worth asking for your money back.

I'd like to have a word with you sometime, about a personal ....

Household rubbish, including paper, glass, plastic and organic .... , should be sorted into separate categories.

27 The local buses charge a .... fare of 70p to the town centre.

Jeff's demand for a meeting with management was met with a .... refusal.

My car battery's completely .... , because I must have left the lights on all night.

28 Suspicion immediately .... on the last person to see the woman before her disappearance.

Their relationship just .... to pieces after they'd only been together for a few months.

As more jobs became available in the improving economic situation, the rate of unemployment .... sharply.

29 Eve set out, armed with a stout stick, to .... a path through clumps of bushes and enormous ferns.

The midday sun .... down mercilessly on the withered crops in the dried-up fields.

Just .... the egg white until it's frothy, and fold it into the mixture.

30 The salesman .... the customer to believe that the car had had only one previous owner.

A narrow path through the wood .... all the way to the back of the hotel.

The former soldier found civilian life boring as he had .... such an exciting life in the army.

31 To call for assistance, ... the bell at the reception desk.

The reporters began to .... the politician for more information about the reasons for his resignation.

The police finally confirmed that they intended to .... charges against both women.

Part 4

For questions **32–39**, complete the second sentence so that it has a similar meaning to the first sentence, using the word given. **Do not change the word given.** You must use between **three** and **eight** words, including the word given.

Here is an example **(0)**.

Example:

0 Do you mind if I watch you while you paint?

objection

Do you .... you while you paint?

0	*have any objection to my watching*

Write **only** the missing words **on the separate answer sheet**.

---

32 The present government has never promised to lower taxation.

time

At .... promised to lower taxation.

33 Helen's report is rather unclear in places.

lacking

Helen's report .... in places.

34 William tried to remain impartial in the quarrel between his two cousins.

sides

William tried .... in the quarrel between his two cousins.

35 Andrew is the most generous person I have ever met.

more

I've yet .... Andrew.

36 Jason didn't hesitate for a moment before he accepted the offer.

slightest

Jason didn't .... accepting the offer.

37 I never thought that I would win a prize.

crossed

It .... that I would win a prize.

38 I don't understand the reason for Liz's sudden departure yesterday.

why

I don't understand .... yesterday.

39 Having explained things three times, Simon's patience was exhausted.

run

Having explained things three times, Simon .... patience.

Part 5

For questions **40–44**, read the following texts on business practice. For questions **40–43**, answer with a word or short phrase. You do not need to write complete sentences. For question **44**, write a summary according to the instructions given.

Write your answers to questions **40–44 on the separate answer sheet**.

Business is becoming more and more a matter of intellectual prowess. Business success is based ever more directly and speedily on the abilities of the people in the business world to change, foresee trends, take acceptable risks, be more in tune with tomorrow's needs of today's customers and to set their stalls out for the myriad **line 4** economic and social changes that are occurring. To seize advantage in these ways is not a matter of brute force, but one of finely honed intelligence, coupled with genuine qualities of character and a continuous dedication to staying ahead in the race. Just as athletics demonstrates continuously that not only does an athlete have to be in good shape but also in the right frame of mind to win, so it is with business. The difficulty is that, while few will contradict these statements, few also follow the logic of their beliefs through to a coherent and consistent philosophy which imbues their company from top to bottom. Nor will you find these issues the subject of endless board debate and introspection. Even companies which have a clearly expressed and understood company style, to which they attribute their company advantage, have come across it more by accident than by planning. Some companies are proud of their restless style of management, which is never satisfied with its achievements, but this characteristic derives as much from the character of the chief executive as from deep philosophical debate.

40 Why is the use of the phrase 'set their stalls out' (line 4) particularly appropriate in this context?

....

41 According to the writer, how are company philosophies arrived at?

....

Successful ambitious companies with clear visions need successful ambitious people who can 'live the vision' for both business and themselves and who see that the two **line 2** go hand in hand. Successful operations result not from working harder but from working more effectively, which in turn is the result not of individual efforts, but of the system in which the individuals work. Group success won by raising the performance of the system automatically increases the success of group members.

The analogy with a sports team is self-evident. Buying an expensive star won't make a bad football team good, but a good side, with a shared vision of excellent performance and how to achieve it, turns mediocre players into star performers. The importance of group vision doesn't diminish the individual role but enhances it. A system in which individuals can correct defects and suggest improvements, including the vision and its fulfilment, will have higher performance and more satisfied, better-motivated people, than one in which they are confined to obeying orders from on **line 13** high. **line 14**

The philosophy hinges on releasing the initiative and ability of companies, teams and individuals to perform better, and to go on raising their game – in short, to make progress, a word conveying the essence of true success and the power of true vision. Not everyone can come first, but anyone can advance closer to important goals, and having reached them can pitch their vision higher still. For companies, teams and individuals, success is never total, for progress can always be made.

42 Explain in your own words what the writer means when he says that successful companies need people who can 'live the vision' (line 2).

....

43 Why might 'obeying orders from on high' (lines 13–14) be detrimental to the development of a business?

....

44 In a paragraph of between **50** and **70** words, summarise **in your own words as far as possible** the comparisons made by the writers between success in business and success in sport. Write your summary **on the separate answer sheet**.

PAPER 4   LISTENING (40 minutes approximately)

Part 1

You will hear four different extracts. For questions **1–8**, choose the answer (**A**, **B** or **C**) which fits best according to what you hear. There are two questions for each extract.

Extract 1

You hear part of a radio interview with Tom Webster, an actor whose latest film has just been released.

1 In Tom's opinion, what may be the reason for an actor's refusal to give an interview?

   A   the actor's dissatisfaction with their performance
   B   the tendency of journalists to ask embarrassing questions
   C   the audience's failure to show interest in the actor's current film

                                                                      1

2 What is Tom's attitude towards today's interview?

   A   He is appreciative of the chance to discuss film-making.
   B   He wants to focus on the film he has made.
   C   He knows the publicity will help his film career.

                                                                      2

Extract 2

You hear a psychologist talking about ways of measuring personality.

3 What does the speaker say about the way we describe people's personality?

   A   It demands a large vocabulary.
   B   It may involve personal feelings.
   C   It can lead to misunderstandings.

                                                                     3

4 The speaker refers to 'extroversion' and 'introversion' to illustrate changes in

   A   how the words are defined.
   B   how personality is analysed.
   C   the way people behave.

                                                                     4

Extract 3

You hear a journalist, who travels for his work, talking about what home means to him.

5 How did the speaker feel when he was growing up in Scotland?

   A   lost
   B   alone
   C   trapped

5

6 What motivated the speaker to try to return to Scotland in later life?

   A   a romantic longing for security
   B   a desire to leave London
   C   a sudden impulse to relive memories

6

Extract 4

You hear part of a radio interview with the author of a new book about the USA.

7 The author had previously decided against writing a book on the USA because

   A   he thought the subject was too broad.
   B   he had not travelled extensively in the country.
   C   he knew the project would require a lot of concentration.

7

8 The author's book consists of material which

   A   represents about half his output on the topic.
   B   was originally published elsewhere.
   C   presents a unified view of the USA.

8

Part 2

You will hear part of a radio programme about ice-skating rinks. For questions **9–17**, complete the sentences with a word or short phrase.

___

Ice-skating was originally used as a way of

| | **9** | around northern European waterways.

The first indoor rinks were popular because they offered skaters a

| | **10** | from the cold.

The spread of indoor rinks was limited by the cost of the piping, made of

| | **11** |

In the second half of the twentieth century,

| | **12** | was added as an event to the Winter Olympics.

The technology used to make the ice for indoor ice rinks is similar to that used in domestic

| | **13** | and refrigeration.

The water for the first two very thin layers of ice is pumped through a

| | **14** |

Sponsors of hockey teams may have their

| | **15** | painted on the ice.

The top layer of ice can take up to

| | **16** | to apply.

The wrong environmental conditions in the building can produce a layer of

| | **17** | above the surface of the ice.

Part 3

You will hear the beginning of a radio interview with Stephen Perrins, a composer of musicals. For questions **18–22**, choose the answer (**A**, **B**, **C** or **D**) which fits best according to what you hear.

18 The light songs Stephen wrote at college weren't published because

    A   he couldn't interest a publisher in them.
    B   he was afraid of people's reactions.
    C   his family advised him against it.
    D   he didn't think they would sell.

| | 18 |

19 Stephen and Jenny's original reason for writing *Goldringer* was that

    A   they wanted to include it in their college show.
    B   it was commissioned for a school concert.
    C   they wanted to find out if they were able to do so.
    D   a music publisher asked them to write a musical.

| | 19 |

20 Stephen prefers not to write the lyrics for his shows because he

    A   would rather work with someone else.
    B   finds it difficult to write them.
    C   thinks they are of poor quality.
    D   is only interested in writing music.

| | 20 |

21 Stephen's purpose in mentioning Helen Downes is to convince listeners that

    A   he has strong views about productions of his musicals.
    B   Helen Downes was an unsuitable director.
    C   the design for a particular show was of too low a standard.
    D   the director has ultimate responsibility for a production.

| | 21 |

22 Stephen claims that the reason why some newspapers criticise him is that

    A   they think he is conceited.
    B   they don't like his music.
    C   he isn't interested in publicity.
    D   he tries to control his public image.

| | 22 |

Part 4

You will hear part of a radio arts programme, in which two people, Arthur and Carla, are discussing a book called *Windworld*. For questions **23–28**, decide whether the opinions are expressed by only one of the speakers, or whether the speakers agree.

Write   **A**   for Arthur,
         C   for Carla,
or   **B**   for Both, where they agree.

---

23   The portrayal of key individuals in the story is confidently handled.   **23**

24   The historical information fits the period in which the novel is set.   **24**

25   The inclusion of too many scientific facts undermines the story.   **25**

26   *Windworld* is aimed at a different audience to that of Swallow's other books.   **26**

27   The story benefits from the inclusion of autobiographical elements.   **27**

28   A film version of this novel should only focus on personal elements.   **28**

PAPER 5   SPEAKING (19 minutes)

There are two examiners. One (the Interlocutor) conducts the test, providing you with the necessary materials and explaining what you have to do. The other examiner (the Assessor) will be introduced to you, but then takes no further part in the interaction.

Part 1 (3 minutes)

The Interlocutor first asks you and your partner a few questions which focus on information about yourselves and personal opinions.

Part 2 (4 minutes)

In this part of the test you and your partner are asked to talk together. The Interlocutor places a set of pictures on the table in front of you. This stimulus provides the basis for a discussion. The Interlocutor first asks an introductory question which focuses on one or two of the pictures. After about a minute, the Interlocutor gives you both a decision-making task based on the same set of pictures.

The pictures for Part 2 are on pages C2–C3 of the colour section.

Part 3 (12 minutes)

You are each given the opportunity to talk for two minutes, to comment after your partner has spoken and to take part in a more general discussion.

The Interlocutor gives you a card with a question written on it and asks you to talk about it for two minutes. After you have spoken, your partner is first asked to comment and then the Interlocutor asks you both another question related to the topic on the card. This procedure is repeated, so that your partner receives a card and speaks for two minutes, you are given an opportunity to comment and a follow-up question is asked.

Finally, the Interlocutor asks some further questions, which leads to a discussion on a general theme related to the subjects already covered in Part 3.

The cards for Part 3 are on pages C10–C11 of the colour section.

Test 2

PAPER 1 READING (1 hour 30 minutes)

Part 1

For questions **1–18**, read the three texts below and decide which answer (**A**, **B**, **C** or **D**) best fits each gap.

Mark your answers **on the separate answer sheet**.

Sand

Much as I admire sand's miraculous ability to be transformed into useful objects like glass and concrete, I am not a great fan of it in its **(1)** .... state. To me it is primarily a hostile barrier that stands between a seaside car park and the water itself. It blows in your face, **(2)** .... in your sandwiches, and swallows vital objects like car keys and coins. When you are wet it **(3)** .... to you like 'stucco', and cannot be **(4)** .... , even with a fireman's hose. But, and here's the strange thing, the moment you step onto a beach towel, climb into a car or walk across a recently vacuumed carpet, it pours off you. For days afterwards, you tip mysteriously undiminishing piles of it onto the floor every time you take off your shoes, and spray the vicinity with lots more when you **(5)** .... your socks. Sand stays with you for longer than many contagious diseases. No, you can **(6)** .... sand, as far as I am concerned.

1	**A**	normal	**B**	natural	**C**	unrefined	**D**	unmixed
2	**A**	enters	**B**	seeps	**C**	gets	**D**	comes
3	**A**	adheres	**B**	attracts	**C**	fixes	**D**	grips
4	**A**	shorn	**B**	scraped	**C**	shoved	**D**	shifted
5	**A**	peel off	**B**	roll away	**C**	move off	**D**	strip away
6	**A**	have	**B**	keep	**C**	hold	**D**	store

Lock and Key

The search for a safe home, for privacy and security, has existed ever since human beings first built a permanent homestead. The rope-lifted beam behind the door may have **(7)** .... to an electronic lock triggered by a plastic card with more combinations than there are atoms in the universe, but the **(8)** .... to shut out the 'bad guys' remains. The appeal of a lock and key is, to some **(9)** .... , psychological. Recently, various companies have experimented with computerised locking systems, where smart cards, swiped through a 'reader', control electronic locks by means of a digital **(10)** .... . But people don't like them. You may be **(11)** .... to put up with it at work, but at home, everyone wants the **(12)** .... of turning a physical key in a lock. As a result, when one locksmith company developed a new electronic system, they made sure they incorporated a proper metal key into the device.

7	**A**	taken on	**B**	given way	**C**	handed down	**D**	passed over
8	**A**	force	**B**	craving	**C**	shove	**D**	urge
9	**A**	extent	**B**	rate	**C**	measure	**D**	scale
10	**A**	directive	**B**	command	**C**	rule	**D**	manipulation
11	**A**	agreeable	**B**	liable	**C**	prepared	**D**	geared
12	**A**	reassurance	**B**	guarantee	**C**	endorsement	**D**	confirmation

Modern Art

I was nervous about visiting the new Tate Modern gallery as, like many people, I can make head nor **(13)** .... of modern art. I know I quite like some of it, furry things in particular, neon light sculptures and massive photographs. Perhaps if I were better informed about it, I'd have an opinion on more things. There again, you're not meant to **(14)** .... about it in a school-essay way. The point is not to grasp art, but to let it communicate with you. This is a splendid idea but one that never worked for me in **(15)** .... . But this new gallery has tried to give the visitor a genuine insight into the whys and wherefores of the works. The first thing I noticed were the labels, proper labels that set a work in **(16)** .... and actually told you what it was trying to say. Instead of staring **(17)** .... at the pictures as I used to, these **(18)** .... of information helped me understand.

13	**A**	foot	**B**	tail	**C**	heart	**D**	heel
14	**A**	set	**B**	look	**C**	start	**D**	put
15	**A**	honesty	**B**	purpose	**C**	practice	**D**	action
16	**A**	context	**B**	place	**C**	contrast	**D**	situation
17	**A**	barely	**B**	clearly	**C**	blankly	**D**	plainly
18	**A**	nuggets	**B**	abstracts	**C**	extracts	**D**	cuttings

Part 2

You are going to read four extracts which are all concerned in some way with group dynamics. For questions **19–26**, choose the answer (**A**, **B**, **C** or **D**) which you think fits best according to the text.

Mark your answers **on the separate answer sheet**.

Observing Lions

In the popular imagination, lions hunting for food present a marvel of group choreography: in the dying light of sunset, a band of stealthy cats springs forth from the shadows like trained assassins and surrounds its unsuspecting prey. The lions seem to be archetypal social animals, rising above petty dissension to work together towards a common goal – in this case, their next meal. But after spending many years observing these creatures in the wild, we have acquired a less exalted view.

When we started our research in 1978, we hoped to discover why lions teamed up   line 7
to hunt, rear cubs and among other things, scare off rivals with chorused roars. If   line 8
the ultimate success of an animal's behaviour is measured by its lifetime production   line 9
of surviving offspring, then cooperation does not necessarily pay: if an animal is too   line 10
generous, its companions benefit at its expense. Why, then, did not the evolutionary   line 11
rules of genetic self-interest seem to apply to lions?   line 12

We confidently assumed that we would be able to resolve that issue in two to three years. But lions are supremely adept at doing nothing. To the list of inert noble gases, including krypton, argon and neon, we would add lion. Thus it has taken a variety of research measures to uncover clues about the cats' behaviour. Because wild lions can live up to 18 years, the answers to our questions are only now becoming clear.

19 In the first paragraph, the writer suggests that the results of his research

    A may not confirm commonly-held opinions.
    B may contradict findings in other studies.
    C will require some unpleasant descriptive writing.
    D will have implications for other social groups.

20 The writer illustrates what he means by 'evolutionary rules' (lines 11–12) when he refers to

    A the fact that 'lions teamed up to hunt'. (lines 7–8)
    B 'the ultimate success of an animal's behaviour'. (line 9)
    C the 'lifetime production of surviving offspring'. (lines 9–10)
    D the fact that 'cooperation does not necessarily pay'. (line 10)

Pop Music Review

The release of Bedrock's third album was more than just a landmark in the career of a talented but hitherto precarious band. *New Life* launched a movement that effectively redesigned the specification of rock music in this country for the rest of the decade. Out went the earnest angst, plain-shirted drabness and overdriven guitars of a previous era; in came a lighter blend of melodious homegrown styles. A mix of social observation and strident anger mingled easily here with the sound of fairground organs and northern brass bands. Humour and irony were well to the fore, as were the voices that felt no need to disguise their origins.

The album showed Bedrock to be skilful magpie collectors and observers, and a cunningly versatile team of songwriters. At their most obvious, they went larkily after traditional English preoccupations such as sunbathing and Sunday afternoons. But the album's real strength lay in the gentle melancholy depths it plumbed on tracks such as 'So Low', a gorgeous unfurling tune loosely hung around the theme of meteorology, and 'To the Brink', a ballad that allowed no smirking at the back. The beauty of *New Life* is its consistently sky-high quality – 16 tracks with absolutely no filler remains an unsurpassed record in the era of loiteringly long CDs.

21   In the writer's view, what was Bedrock's musical status prior to the release of *New Life*?

  A   They had been overlooked by music experts.
  B   Their music did not fit with any particular genre.
  C   Their foothold in the music world had been uncertain.
  D   They had been unable to successfully mix style and image.

22   The writer suggests that *New Life* outshines other albums of its time because

  A   the collection of songs successfully combines wit and sentiment.
  B   the lyrics portray situations that are known to its listeners.
  C   all the band members contributed to its construction.
  D   every track that it features is worth listening to.

Extract from an autobiography

As a child I was always fascinated by stories of 'The Sibyl', those mysteriously wise
women who wielded such influence in the ancient world. To begin with, I only knew of
the existence of one who appeared in a tale my mother had told me. An old woman of
Cumae offered Tarquin, King of Rome, nine books for 300 gold pieces. He refused and
she burnt three of them, offering him six for the same price. When he refused, she again
burnt three books. He bought the remaining three for the full 300 gold pieces.

I realised even then that there was a profound truth hidden in the story – a lesson in
salesmanship and in life. I was sometimes a lonely only child. I used to ask to play with
other children and be refused. My mother told me to do something so interesting that all
the other kids would beg to join me. It worked. It was another lesson that I've never
forgotten.

When I was given the chance to write a travel book, I had to look for something that I
could bear to find out about, something that was relevant to my life. I'm a reluctant
traveller – at the first opportunity I sent my editor a very long list of places I wasn't
prepared to go to. When it comes down to it, I'm only interested in ruins, because the travel
I like is the travel of the mind through time.

23   What impressed the writer about the story of the old woman?

   A   It provided her with a model of behaviour.
   B   It underpinned her moral standpoint.
   C   It illustrated a common misconception.
   D   It gave her a salutary warning.

24   What was the writer's attitude towards writing a travel book?

   A   She was worried about the time commitment involved.
   B   She was unwilling to go to certain places unprepared.
   C   She challenged her editor's initial suggestions.
   D   She insisted on following her own inclinations.

What becomes of your manuscript?

When you submit your manuscript it will most likely join a heap waiting for someone to sort and sift before it topples over – the so-called slush pile. The someone is usually either the editorial department junior (i.e. under 18) or an old hand who comes in a couple of mornings a week and is paid by the hour. Neither of these has much influence, but they are basically on your side and out to discover something original – the junior to make his or her name and acquire an author of their own if they are lucky, the old hand to justify continuing freelance employment.

If they think your novel is promising, they will pass it on to a more senior editor and eventually it will surface at an acquisition meeting. The championing editor will not only have to justify accepting your novel on the grounds of intrinsic merit and potential sales, but also say whether you as an author seem to be a long-term prospect (which you will have assured them of in your letter). Also the question is raised of how promotable you are likely to be – an important factor in an age when a new novel needs all the help it can get. To this end,   **line 15** publishers often like to meet a potential author before clinching the offer.

25 What encouraging information does the writer offer to authors who submit manuscripts to publishers?

   A   Manuscripts are often dealt with quickly.
   B   The staff are keen to identify a new author.
   C   A well-written novel will definitely be noticed.
   D   The initial selection process is very thorough.

26 What does the phrase 'To this end' (line 15) refer to?

   A   assessing an author's publicity value
   B   predicting a novel's commercial success
   C   judging the appearance of a novel
   D   evaluating an author's loyalty to a publisher

Part 3

You are going to read a newspaper article about sleep. Seven paragraphs have been removed from the article. Choose from the paragraphs **A–H** the one which fits each gap (**27–33**). There is one extra paragraph which you do not need to use.

Mark your answers **on the separate answer sheet**.

Enough Sleep?

Tiredness, it is often claimed, has become the modern condition. As the richer, busier countries have grown, so sleeplessness and anxiety have also grown in the popular psyche. Research in the USA has found 40 million Americans to be chronically affected, and some recent best-selling novels in Britain have featured insomniacs as protagonists, or sleep-research laboratories as their settings.

| 27 | |

Recently, a sleep researcher tried an experiment. He offered his subjects the opposite of the modern routine. 'I allowed them to sleep for up to 14 hours a night for a month. It took them three weeks to reach an equilibrium of eight-and-a-quarter hours. That indicates a great rebound of sleep – sleep that they hadn't been getting.'

| 28 | |

For guinea pigs, they advertise in the student newspapers. Subjects are picked up by taxi, paid £5 an hour, and asked to adjust their sleeping patterns according to instructions. Dr Louise Reyner provides reassurance: 'Some people are quite worried, because you're putting electrodes on their heads, and they think you can see what they're dreaming or thinking.'

| 29 | |

The young men all deny they are going to fall asleep. Dr Reyner has a video recording of one trying not to. At first the person at the wheel is very upright, wet and bleary eyes determinedly fixed on the windscreen. Then he begins to blink briefly, every now and again; then for longer, and more often, with a slight drop of the head. Each nod grows heavier than the last. The blinks become a 10-second blackout. Every time, he jerks awake as if nothing has happened. But the car, by the second or third occasion, has shot off the carriageway.

| 30 | |

But apart from these findings, what else do we know about human sleep with any kind of certainty? It is known that humans sleep, like other mammals, according to a daily cycle. Once asleep, they switch between four different stages of unconsciousness, from stage one sleep, the shallowest, to stage four, the deepest. When dreams occur, which is usually during the lightest sleep, the brain paralyses the body except for the hands and eyelids, thus preventing injuries.

| 31 | |

However, there is a strong degree of certainty among scientists that women sleep for half an hour longer than men, and that older people require less sleep, though they don't know why. When asked what sleep is for, some sleep researchers reply in cosmic terms: 'Sleep is a tactic to travel through time without injury.'

32

The interlude was a haven for reflection, remembering dreams, or even night-time thieving. The poorest were the greatest beneficiaries of this quiet time, fleetingly freed from the constraints and labours that ruled their day-time existence.

33

Yet beyond Europe and America, the old pattern was widespread until quite recently, and according to a leading anthropologist, in some non-western settings there are still no rigid bedtimes. People go to bed for a few hours, and then get up again. The idea of a night's solid sleep does not apply. For certain tribal societies, human and animal noises and the need to supervise the fire and watch out for predators combine to make continuous sleep impossible. It seems that people all round the world are badly in need of sleep.

A Beyond this, certainties blur into theories. It is often suggested, for example, that sleep repairs body tissue, or restores muscles, or rests the frontal section of the brain that controls speech and creativity. But all of this may happen more quickly during relaxed wakefulness, so no one is really sure.

B Part of this interest is in sleep in general: in its rhythms, its uses and in problems with sleeping. But a central preoccupation remains. 'People need more sleep,' says one leading sleep researcher. 'People cut back on sleep when they're busy. They get up too early to avoid the rush hour.'

C By the 17th century, however, as artificial light became more common, the rich began to switch to the more concentrated, and economically more efficient, mode of re-cuperation that we follow today. Two centuries later, the industrial revolution pushed back the dusk for everyone except some country-dwellers, by making most people work longer hours in lighted buildings.

D The sleep researchers seem interested in this theory. But the laboratory is not funded to investigate such matters. Its sponsors want its research to lead to practical solutions such as deciding where *Take a Break* signs should be placed on motorways, and how different kinds of food and drink can affect driving and sleepiness.

E A coffee might have helped. Two cups, Dr Reyner says, even after no sleep at all,

can make you a safe driver for half an hour or more. She recommends a whole basket of alertness products: tablets, energy drinks, caffeinated chewing gum. Shift workers, she is quite sure, could probably use them.

F Moreover, people may have had different sleep patterns in the past. A history professor has investigated nocturnal British life between 1500 and 1850 and discovered that sleeping routines were very different. People went to bed at nine or ten, then woke up after midnight, after what they called their 'first sleep', stayed awake for an hour, and then had their 'morning sleep'.

G In fact, the laboratory's interest is more physical. In a darkened room stands a motorway simulator, the front section of a car facing a wide projection screen. The subjects are always told to arrive at 2pm, in the body's natural mid-afternoon lull, after a short night's sleep or no sleep at all. The projector is switched on and they are asked to drive, while answering questions. An endless road rolls ahead, sunlight glares; and the air is warm.

H In Europe, such propositions are perhaps most thoroughly tested in a small, unassuming building on a university campus in the English Midlands. The university sleep research laboratory has investigated, among many subjects, the effects of fatigue on sailors, the effects of airport noise on sleepers, and the dangers of motorway driving for flagging drivers.

Part 4

You are going to read an extract from a textbook. For questions **34–40**, choose the answer (**A**, **B**, **C** or **D**) which you think fits best according to the text.

Mark your answers **on the separate answer sheet**.

BROADCASTING: The Social Shaping of a Technology

'Broadcasting' originally meant sowing seeds broadly, by hand. It is, in other words, not only an agricultural metaphor, it is also one of optimistic modernism. It is about   **line 2** planned growth in the widest possible circles, the production, if the conditions are right,   **line 3** of a rich harvest. The metaphor presupposes a bucket of seeds at the centre of the activity,   **line 4** i.e. the existence of centralised resources intended and suited for spreading – and   **line 5** reproduction. The question to be looked into is why a new technology that transmitted words and pictures electronically was organised in a way that made this agricultural metaphor seem adequate.

Since television as a technology is related to various two-way forms of communication, such as the telegraph and the telephone, it is all the more striking that, from its very early days, it was envisaged as a centralised 'mass' medium. However, transmission to private homes from some centralised unit was simply in keeping with both socio-economic structures and the dominant ways of life in modern and modernising societies. Attempts or experiments with other forms of organisation in the long run remained just that – attempts and experiments. Two little-known, distinct alternatives deserve mentioning since they highlight what television might have been – in a different social context.

Experiments with two-way television as a possible replacement for the ordinary telephone were followed up, so to speak, by radio amateurs in Britain in the early 1930s. Various popular science journals, such as *Radio News*, had detailed articles about how to construct television transmitters and receivers and, throughout the 1930s, experimenting amateurs were active in many parts of the country. But Big Business, represented by the British Radio Manufacturers Association, in 1938 agreed upon standards for television equipment and channel regulations which drove the grass-roots activists out. And so there passed, at least in Britain, the historical 'moment' for a counter-cultural development of television as a widely diffused, grass-roots, egalitarian form of communication.

Broadcasting in some form was, however, tied not only to strong economic interests, but also to the deep structures of modern societies. In spite of the activities of TV amateurs, television was also primarily a medium for theatrical exhibition in the USA in the early 1930s, and as such often thought to be a potential competitor of the film industry. In fact, television was throughout the 1930s predominantly watched in public settings also outside of the USA. For example, in Britain, *public* viewing of television was the way in which most early audiences actually experienced the medium and this was even more the case in Germany. While the vision of grass-roots or amateur, two-way television was quite obviously doomed to a very marginal position at the very best, television systems largely based on collective public reception were in fact operating in several countries in the 1930s and may, with the benefit of hindsight, be seen as having presented more of a threat to the domestication of the medium. But it was a threat that was not to materialise.

Manufacturers saw the possibilities for mass sales of domestic sets as soon as the price could be reduced, and given the division and relation between the public and private domains fundamental to modernity, centralised broadcasting to a dispersed domestic audience was clearly the most adequate organisation of the medium. As working-class people achieved improved standards of living and entered 'consumer' society from about the 1920s onwards, the dreams of the home as a fully equipped centre for entertainment and diverse cultural experiences became realisable for the majority of inhabitants of Western nation-states. And all of this is now also happening on a global scale.

There is a clear relationship between the basic processes of social modernisation and the dominant structures of broadcasting. While social and economic modernisation meant increasing centralisation and concentration of capital and political power, the break-up of traditional communities produced new ways of life. Mobility was both social and geographical, and both forms implied that individuals and households were, both literally and metaphorically, 'on the move' in ways that left them relatively isolated compared to people in much more stable early communities. Centralised broadcasting was both an answer to the need felt by central government to reach all citizens with important information efficiently, and a highly useful instrument in the production of the harmonising, stabilising 'imagined community' of the nation-state.

The pervasiveness of these structured processes and interests rendered broadcasting the 'naturally' victorious organisation of both radio and television. What is left out here is the more positive view of broadcasting as a social form suitable also for democracy. In the formation of broadcasting policies between the World Wars, the interest in broadcasting as a means of securing equal access to resources necessary for conscious, informed and autonomous participation in political, social and cultural life played a very important role in many countries. Of course television is changing, and there is the risk that the very term broadcasting becomes outmoded or at least inadequate. In which case, this metaphor will be seen only as referring to a particular organisation of audio-visual technology during a certain centralised phase of social modernisation.

34 In the metaphor explored by the writer in the first paragraph, what does the 'bucket of seeds' (line 4) represent?

  A planned growth (line 3)
  B a rich harvest (line 4)
  C the centre of the activity (line 4)
  D centralised resources (line 5)

35 In the second paragraph, what view does the writer express about the way in which television developed?

    A It confirmed the results of experiments.
    B It reflected other social trends.
    C It was dominated by other technologies.
    D It was limited by economic constraints.

36 The writer regards the experiments by radio amateurs in the 1930s as

    A a missed opportunity to use television technology in a different way.
    B investigations into the commercial potential of television technology.
    C a breakthrough in the development of new types of television transmitters.
    D attempts to establish a more effective means of communication than the telephone.

37 Looking back, what does the writer feel about public viewings of TV in the 1930s?

    A They received a lot of opposition from the film industry.
    B They were limited to small audiences outside the USA.
    C They might have provided an alternative to the way broadcasting developed.
    D They were less significant than the experiments with two-way television.

38 Transmission to people's homes became a dominant feature of television because

    A changes in society had created a demand for this.
    B it became possible to manufacture televisions on a domestic scale.
    C television audiences were seen as potential consumers of advertised goods.
    D it was an effective way of delivering the programme schedules that people wanted.

39 In the sixth paragraph, the writer says that the authorities saw broadcasting as a means of

    A controlling the information that people received.
    B accelerating the process of modernisation.
    C boosting their own political influence.
    D counteracting social upheaval.

40 In the final paragraph, what does the writer say he has omitted from his earlier analysis?

    A The factors that motivate people in the broadcasting industry.
    B The resources needed to operate a broadcasting service.
    C The capacity of broadcasting to empower people.
    D The strength of the interests behind broadcasting.

PAPER 2   WRITING (2 hours)

Part 1

You **must** answer this question. Write your answer in **300–350** words in an appropriate style.

---

1   You see the following two letters printed in a magazine.

> I never want to grow old because then you have nothing
> to offer society, and other people have to look after you
> and worry about you.
>
> ADRIAN (18 YEARS OLD)

> I love being the age I am (over 60) because now I am free to
> enjoy life and do all the things I have always wanted to do. I
> have learnt a lot about life, and I have a lot to offer other
> people. Life is great.
>
> JANE (62 YEARS OLD)

The magazine is inviting readers to express their views on the subject of growing old. You decide to write a letter to the magazine, responding to the points raised and expressing your own views.

Write your **letter**. Do not write any postal addresses.

Part 2

Write an answer to **one** of the questions **2–5** in this part. Write your answer in **300–350** words in an appropriate style.

---

2 You read the following in an international magazine:

> Poverty exists in almost every country, and the difference between the rich and the poor is growing all the time. What can we do about this situation?

The magazine has asked people to send in ideas in the form of a proposal, suggesting ways of helping to reduce poverty. You decide to send in a proposal.

Write your **proposal**.

3 The local council has conducted a survey to find out if local residents think that public money should be spent on a new leisure centre, a new library or a new playground for children. You have been asked to write a report for the local council based on the opinions the residents gave in the survey, and make appropriate recommendations.

Write your **report**.

4 *International Traveller* magazine is running a competition for the best article entitled 'A Country of Contrasts'. You decide to submit an entry. The article should describe the contrasts that make the country an interesting place to visit, and encourage the readers to explore the country as widely as possible.

Write your **article**.

5 Based on your reading of **one** of these books, write on **one** of the following.

(a) Anne Tyler: *The Accidental Tourist*
'A dried-up kernel of a man that nothing really penetrates.' Write an essay for your tutor in which you say how far you agree with this view of Macon.

Write your **essay**.

(b) John Wyndham: *The Day of the Triffids*
The editor of a literary magazine is asking for reviews of books which describe events that changed the world. You write a review of *The Day of the Triffids* in which you describe the events and say whether or not the book gives an optimistic view of human nature.

Write your **review**.

(c) Graham Greene: *Our Man in Havana*
'*Our Man in Havana* was written to amuse and entertain the reader. It has no serious moral purpose.' Write an essay for your tutor, saying how far you agree or disagree with this view of the novel.

Write your **essay**.

Part 3

For questions **26–31**, think of **one** word only which can be used appropriately in all three sentences. Here is an example **(0)**.

Example:

0 Some of the tourists are hoping to get compensation for the poor state of the hotel, and I think they have a very .... case.

There's no point in trying to wade across the river, the current is far too ....

If you're asking me which of the candidates should get the job, I'm afraid I don't have any .... views either way.

0	S	T	R	O	N	G														

Write **only** the missing word in CAPITAL LETTERS **on the separate answer sheet**.

---

26 This jacket's a bit .... in the sleeves; I think you should try another one.

Try to avoid annoying Richard, because he's got a very .... temper.

Lucy was rather .... of breath after climbing the 350 steps to the top of the tower.

27 The texture of this fabric is quite .... to the touch.

Many passengers were ill, since the sea was quite .... during the crossing.

The architect produced a .... sketch of his plans for the new houses.

28 With this new householder's policy, we are .... against fire and theft.

The stone carving they found in the jungle was .... by a thick layer of mud.

On the first day after leaving camp, the explorers .... only ten kilometres.

29 As soon as the boat .... the shore, Ben leapt quickly out and hauled it up.

When Sally opened her present she was very .... by her parents' generosity.

When Jim accidentally .... the switch, the alarm went off, much to his consternation.

30 Now that Tom has so little time, how does he keep .... of all his investments?

Although the .... they found through the wood was narrow, it turned out to be easy to follow.

The station is no longer used and the railway .... has become overgrown with weeds.

31 It's not a .... of whether we want to go on holiday, but whether we can afford it.

Amy's loyalty is not in .... , since we have complete faith in her.

Apart from the obvious .... of space, do you think the club really needs new premises?

Part 4

For questions **32–39**, complete the second sentence so that it has a similar meaning to the first sentence, using the word given. **Do not change the word given**. You must use between **three** and **eight** words, including the word given.

Here is an example **(0)**.

Example:

0 Do you mind if I watch you while you paint?

objection

Do you .... you while you paint?

0	*have any objection to my watching*

Write **only** the missing words **on the separate answer sheet**.

---

32 I really enjoy reading, but sometimes I feel like doing something more active.

times

Much .... I prefer to do something more active.

33 The president only made his formal announcement after the publication of the leaked information.

did

Not until the leaked information .... his formal announcement.

34 Without your support, I'd never have been able to find a new job.

still

If it hadn't .... doing my old job.

35 The villagers said they opposed the plans for the new shopping centre.

disapproval

The villagers .... the plans for the new shopping centre.

36 I wasn't at all surprised when I heard that Sophie had been promoted.

hear

It came .... Sophie's promotion.

37 I think it would be best if you didn't mention John's behaviour to his mother.

say

I don't think you .... John's behaviour to his mother.

38 I have no idea whatsoever why Zoe resigned from her job.

loss

I am .... why Zoe resigned from her job.

39 The Prime Minister resigned because of his sudden illness.

resulted

The Prime .... his sudden illness.

Part 5

For questions **40–44**, read the following texts on walking in the countryside. For questions **40–43**, answer with a word or short phrase. You do not need to write complete sentences. For question **44**, write a summary according to the instructions given.

Write your answers to questions **40–44 on the separate answer sheet**.

In April I dig out my walking boots. My wife's heart sinks, and a look of cold fury clouds her lovely features. My children laugh scornfully and call me 'so sad' – the two most critical words in the teenage lexicon.

Find those boots I must. Other men smoke like chimneys or follow football teams to Brazil and back. My hopeless addiction is taking long walks. I am, in short, an incurable rambler.

The boots have been hibernating in a cupboard since October, like a couple of curiously-shaped muddy tortoises. Oddly, my rambling compulsion is totally resistible in winter. I know of masochists who stride doggedly over mountainsides while January gales lash their waterproofs and turn their ears blue. For me, the sun must have made some slight attempt to rise above the horizon before I feel a stirring to strike out for the distant countryside.

When I do ramble, boy, do I go on and on! Not for me the gentle stroll around some local country park. It must be some inordinately long, exhausting challenge in the untouched wilderness. It is easy to get depressed about how much of the country is disappearing under concrete and tarmac. I cannot underestimate the damage being done by the relentless march of housebuilders, but ramblers know,   **line 17** even in this overcrowded country, there are extensive tracts where you wander for hours without seeing another soul, gulping in the exhilarating fresh air, just to see what is beyond the next ridge.

40   Explain in your own words the reaction of the writer's family to his hobby.

....

41   Why does the writer describe the 'march of housebuilders' (line 17) as 'relentless'?

....

Researchers have explored the reasons why so many people indulge in outdoor leisure pursuits, such as hiking, in the natural environment. In general, such individuals appear to have less need for affiliation with others, and a preference for solitude as well as high levels of autonomy.

It is possible to make some observations about motivation from this. There is the need for peace and relief of tension facilitated by solitude, and encountering others in the wilderness reduces satisfaction. Then there is confidence building achieved by trying out new activities and acquiring new skills, such as skiing and survival techniques. These can form an important part of an individual's self-concept and improve self-esteem. Stimulation can be obtained by a change in scene, and an opportunity to indulge in risky activities will enhance this, as in the adrenalin rush associated with activities such as bungee jumping. Finally, the natural environment may provide a spiritual uplift, either due to the qualities of the scenery or the symbolic connotations of nature as the giver of life.

Thus, considerable benefits can be gained from outdoor activities, and a range of facilities should be provided to meet the needs of the users. Nevertheless, user satisfaction declines greatly when the outdoor environment is overcrowded or polluted. The necessary facilities must be provided in sufficient quantity as well as   **line 18**
quality.   **line 19**

42   What does the writer suggest about the personality of hikers?

....

43   Explain in your own words why leisure facilities need to be 'provided in sufficient quantity as well as quality'. (lines 18–19)

....

44   In a paragraph of **50–70 words**, summarise **in your own words as far as possible** what, according to the writers of the texts, makes people want to explore the countryside. Write your summary **on the separate answer sheet**.

PAPER 4   LISTENING (40 minutes approximately)

Part 1

You will hear four different extracts. For questions **1–8**, choose the answer (**A**, **B** or **C**) which fits best according to what you hear. There are two questions for each extract.

Extract 1

You hear part of an interview with Nigel Johnson, a writer who has also written and directed films.

1 What was the Irish literary community's reaction to Nigel making a film?

   A   They were jealous of his success.
   B   They thought film-making was beneath him.
   C   They were unhappy at how the film would affect Ireland's image.

2 How does Nigel describe the role of literature in Ireland?

   A   radical
   B   restrictive
   C   professional

Extract 2

You hear a woman telling a friend about two apologies she has received.

3 The common feature of the two anecdotes is that both people apologised

   A   on behalf of someone else.
   B   because they had made a mistake.
   C   without attempting to justify themselves.

4 The woman's anecdotes illustrate that

   A   apologising can stop other people from feeling angry.
   B   people feel better after apologising for their errors.
   C   mistakes seem to be becoming more common these days.

Extract 3

You hear part of a radio documentary entitled *How Laughter Works*.

5   John Morreall believes that laughter may indicate

    A   an inability to deal with fear.
    B   the need to break the ice.
    C   a feeling of ease in a social situation.

6   According to Morreall, some bosses use humour in order to

    A   be flattered by subordinates.
    B   manipulate subordinates' behaviour.
    C   gain the respect of subordinates.

Extract 4

You hear a TV presenter talking about a programme he has worked on.

7   The presenter was unsure about working on the programme because

    A   he didn't know the programme's producer.
    B   he was familiar with the co-presenter's work.
    C   he had doubts about the finished product.

8   One criticism of the pilot programme was

    A   the pace proved to be too slow at one point.
    B   the presenters over-acted their lines.
    C   the subject failed to catch viewers' attention.

Part 2

You will hear an engineer giving a talk on the radio about future developments in robot design. For questions **9–17**, complete the sentences with a word or short phrase.

Currently the field of

	9

is providing aerodynamic information for robot design.

In the past, using the

	10

was the only way scientists could study birds in flight.

The way birds flapped their wings and the arrangement of their

	11

were believed to be the keys to flight.

Scientists are using the design of a

	12

to help them build a small robot.

The flying robot could provide the

	13

with photographs of the interiors of collapsed buildings.

The flying robot must move at

	14

in order to avoid hitting things.

The size of the flying robot means that the

	15

will have to fit in a small space.

Planes were ruled out as models for the flying robot because of the velocity needed for

	16

Engineers rejected helicopters as models for the flying robot because of the issue of

	17

made during flight.

Part 3

You will hear a radio interview with a music critic, Hazel Fisher, about some classical music awards. For questions **18–22**, choose the answer (**A**, **B**, **C** or **D**) which fits best according to what you hear.

___

18 According to Hazel, what is bad about the current situation in the music business?

    A Fewer small record companies are issuing classical music.
    B Publicity is generally concentrated on too few performers.
    C Many good recordings are no longer available.
    D Record companies cannot find good new performers.

    18

19 In Hazel's opinion the list of nominations suggested that a purpose of the awards was to

    A take advantage of current fashions in music.
    B publicise small record companies.
    C strengthen the promotion of serious music.
    D compartmentalise different types of music.

    19

20 What is Hazel's main criticism of the way the winners will be chosen?

    A The voters are unrepresentative of the music industry.
    B The voters have a vested interest in the results.
    C The voting is too time-consuming.
    D The voting system is too complicated.

    20

21 One of Hazel's objections to the nominations themselves is that

    A the criteria for making them were kept secret.
    B they reflect too narrow a definition of music.
    C they are too different to be comparable.
    D there is none of a high enough standard.

    21

22 Hazel sees it as ironic that the record companies

    A are inconsistent about what they consider classical music.
    B have spent so much on the awards while claiming to be short of money.
    C are attempting to popularise music that has little appeal.
    D have introduced their own awards ceremony after condemning others.

    22

Part 4

You will hear two neighbours, Graham and Melinda, discussing changes that the town council are making to a public park near their homes. For questions **23–28**, decide whether the opinions are expressed by only one of the speakers, or whether the speakers agree.

Write **G** for Graham,

       M for Melinda,

or   **B** for Both, where they agree.

23   The town council's action is contrary to the original owner's wishes.   **23**

24   Late-night events will disturb local residents' sleep.   **24**

25   Parking problems will be aggravated by the development.   **25**

26   There was not enough consultation with residents before the plans were put into action.   **26**

27   Commercial interests may have influenced the council's decision to proceed with the plan.   **27**

28   It is now too late to prevent the work being completed.   **28**

PAPER 5   SPEAKING (19 minutes)

There are two examiners. One (the Interlocutor) conducts the test, providing you with the necessary materials and explaining what you have to do. The other examiner (the Assessor) will be introduced to you, but then takes no further part in the interaction.

Part 1 (3 minutes)

The Interlocutor first asks you and your partner a few questions which focus on information about yourselves and personal opinions.

Part 2 (4 minutes)

In this part of the test you and your partner are asked to talk together. The Interlocutor places a set of pictures on the table in front of you. This stimulus provides the basis for a discussion. The Interlocutor first asks an introductory question which focuses on one or two of the pictures. After about a minute, the Interlocutor gives you both a decision-making task based on the same set of pictures.

The pictures for Part 2 are on pages C4–C5 of the colour section.

Part 3 (12 minutes)

You are each given the opportunity to talk for two minutes, to comment after your partner has spoken and to take part in a more general discussion.

The Interlocutor gives you a card with a question written on it and asks you to talk about it for two minutes. After you have spoken, your partner is first asked to comment and then the Interlocutor asks you both another question related to the topic on the card. This procedure is repeated, so that your partner receives a card and speaks for two minutes, you are given an opportunity to comment and a follow-up question is asked.

Finally, the Interlocutor asks some further questions, which leads to a discussion on a general theme related to the subjects already covered in Part 3.

The cards for Part 3 are on pages C10–C11 of the colour section.

Test 3

PAPER 1   READING (1 hour 30 minutes)

Part 1

For questions **1–18**, read the three texts below and decide which answer (**A, B, C** or **D**) best fits each gap.

Mark your answers **on the separate answer sheet**.

___

Metals

It may have been a wish for self-adornment that **(1)** .... the interest of Stone Age people in metals. Sitting by the side of a river, waiting for a fish to come within a spear's throw, or just **(2)** .... away a moment, one of our early ancestors might have happened upon a shiny yellow pebble and plucked it off the river **(3)** .... . It did not have the feel of stone, but it was attractive. In such a way, one could **(4)** .... that gold entered the lives of primitive people.

(5) .... the malleability of the metal, it very soon became a much sought-after material. Copper may also have been discovered by accident, and once the value of copper tools was realised, the search for its ores and for ways of getting the copper out of them was **(6)** .... with vigour. Thus, metalworking was added to our ancestors' battery of life-enhancing accomplishments.

1	**A**	aroused	**B**	enlivened	**C**	cultivated	**D** incited
2	**A**	passing	**B**	idling	**C**	occupying	**D** employing
3	**A**	track	**B**	bed	**C**	floor	**D** path
4	**A**	conjecture	**B**	disclose	**C**	fabricate	**D** prophesy
5	**A**	Providing	**B**	Thanks	**C**	Given	**D** Resulting
6	**A**	raced	**B**	chased	**C**	tracked	**D** pursued

St Ives

There was silence as we **(7)** .... our bags down the winding, cobbled lane that led to the heart of town, **(8)** .... double against the force eight gale and trying in vain to avoid the icy waves that **(9)** .... over the promenade. There was no one on the streets and the shutters in every cottage on the waterfront were bolted tight against the battering. We had watched the weather worsen as we chugged into St Ives on the tiny single-track railway. As the ominous grey skies **(10)** .... in, visiting Cornwall in the off-season – without a car – no longer seemed such a good idea. I had **(11)** .... my friend into joining me with the **(12)** .... of walks along the beautiful Cornish coast, and snug evenings, toasting ourselves before open fires.

7	**A**	lugged	**B**	clambered	**C**	grabbed	**D**	lumbered
8	**A**	leant	**B**	bent	**C**	sloped	**D**	borne
9	**A**	smashed	**B**	engulfed	**C**	splattered	**D**	erupted
10	**A**	folded	**B**	came	**C**	closed	**D**	blew
11	**A**	drawn	**B**	lured	**C**	trapped	**D**	led
12	**A**	provision	**B**	project	**C**	proposal	**D**	promise

Computer Modelling

The problem with studying the past is that it is past. The people who **(13)** .... in times of peace and plenty and struggled through conflict and drought are long dead. The forces that **(14)** .... them to settle here or move there, that brought them together as families and clans, villages and cities, have **(15)** .... from memory. Archaeology provides **(16)** .... and clues, but we cannot test our hypotheses with experiments on cultures living or dead. We cannot rewind the tape and watch a replay of the past. Then again, perhaps we can.

Computer modelling allows us to recreate prehistoric landscapes and environments and **(17)** .... them with virtual communities – digital creations with some of the needs, independence and capabilities of real-world humans. We can establish **(18)** .... of conduct and replicate social units. Then we can turn down the rainfall – or turn up the population – and watch how this cyber-culture and its artificial people react.

13	**A**	endured	**B**	enriched	**C**	prevailed	**D**	prospered
14	**A**	sought	**B**	made	**C**	drove	**D**	chose
15	**A**	dissolved	**B**	faded	**C**	lapsed	**D**	slipped
16	**A**	hints	**B**	tips	**C**	prompts	**D**	cribs
17	**A**	fulfil	**B**	inhabit	**C**	populate	**D**	settle
18	**A**	etiquette	**B**	ways	**C**	manners	**D**	rules

Part 2

You are going to read four extracts which are all concerned in some way with language and literature. For questions **19–26**, choose the answer (**A**, **B**, **C** or **D**) which you think fits best according to the text.

Mark your answers **on the separate answer sheet**.

How to Write Poetry

Telling people how to write poetry is a bit like frolicking through a minefield; spontaneity is the order of the day, but one false step and a dozen certainties will blow up in your face. Setting oneself up as a know-all is dangerous, so I have decided to side-step the whole issue by saying that, for someone just beginning to write, no advice can be a substitute for abundant reading, extensive writing, and the freeing of the imagination and spirit in whatever way seems fruitful, barring total anarchy. Some people need their life to be reasonably secure before a poem will come; others can write their way out of misery. Some write to a timetable; others wait for some moment of crystallisation, a brainwave or slow dawning. All are right, providing they are not echoing some prescriptive score. And it's this **line 10** finding of a tune which is important, hearing the still small voice inside yourself, and feeding it, and watering it, and letting it out for air from time to time; one day it'll be old enough to take care of itself.

19 How does the writer feel about advising people on how to write poetry?

    A   nervous because she feels unqualified to do so
    B   unhappy at being asked
    C   wary of giving misleading guidance
    D   anxious to keep poetry spontaneous

20 What is the writer emphasising when she says 'not echoing some prescriptive score' (line 10)?

    A   the need for originality
    B   the influence of music
    C   the search for inspiration
    D   the nature of insight

The Short Story

In the short story there is no room for overcrowding with too many characters, slabs of lengthy narrative, prolonged reminiscence or retrospection. Flashbacks must be fleeting, and only used if there is no other way to throw light on an issue. One effective way to do this is through a flash of memory in the leading character's mind; the recollection or reminder of an incident or scene, which stirred the current conflict. Such a recollection can get the story on its way or take it a big step forward at a crucial moment, but never at any time must it be allowed to put a brake on the action. In this respect, dialogue is more useful than many aspiring authors realise. Two voices in discussion can reveal two sides of a question in far less time than it takes to explain it from only one person's viewpoint. It also avoids unnecessary wordage and holds or increases a reader's interest. Overwriting can kill a short story from the start, but this doesn't mean that brevity must reduce it to the level of a synopsis. Conflict and action must be as well sustained in a short story as in a novel, but in the short story the art lies in making every word count in a compact space.

21   According to the writer, flashbacks are used because they

    A   can help clarify the characters' reactions.
    B   are a useful device for keeping the story moving.
    C   can remind the reader of how the lead character thinks.
    D   are the best way of throwing light on an incident.

22   According to the text, a short story writer should

    A   use words judiciously.
    B   cut back on some of the action.
    C   try to use dialogue frequently.
    D   keep the reader in suspense.

Screenplays

Anyone who knows how to play chess will understand how to write a screenplay for a film. Most chess players stumble from beginning to end. We don't know much, but we know enough to play. We move without really knowing what's going to happen further on in the game. Maybe we can see one or two moves ahead, and, if we can, we're pleased by our uncanny ability to see even that far ahead. Better than the days when we couldn't see ahead at all – when we were playing blindly.

Over time, as we learned more about playing chess, we made a startling revelation: chess depends more upon long-term strategy than upon short-term tactics. Up till then, we'd been happy with a rather short-sighted approach. Suddenly, we became aware of 'the big picture'. We began to see the game as a whole, not just a series of individual moves. And once we saw the game as a whole, we began to see patterns emerge in the play. Gambits, they call them. And the patterns have names, such as openings, middle games and end games. In chess, as in screenplay writing, the more often you play, the more aware you become of its complexities.

23 According to the writer, how do inexperienced chess players feel?

    A   delighted to be able to finish a game
    B   encouraged by each improvement
    C   amazed by how quickly they learn
    D   pleased to be able to play with confidence

24 The writer compares chess and screenplay writing in order to

    A   explain that we learn both by trial and error.
    B   emphasise the fixed nature of both processes.
    C   suggest that success depends on attention to detail.
    D   demonstrate the importance of having a plan.

Looking at Writing

'Man has an instinctive tendency to speak, as we see in the babble of our young children; while no child has an instinctive tendency to bake, brew, or write.' More than a century ago, Charles Darwin got it right: language is a human instinct, but written language is not. Language is found in all societies, present and past. Although languages change, they do not improve: English is no more complex than the languages of Stone Age tribes; modern English is not an advance of Old English. All healthy children master their language without lessons or corrections. When children are thrown together without a usable language, they invent one of their own. Compare all this with writing.

Writing systems have been invented only infrequently in history. They originated only in a few complex civilisations and they started off crude and slowly improved over the millennia. Until recently, most children never learned to read or write; even with today's universal education, many children struggle and fail. A group of children is no more likely to invent an alphabet than it is to invent the internal combustion engine. Children are wired for sound, but print is an optional accessory that must be painstakingly bolted on. We need to understand how the contraption called writing works, how the minds of the children work, how to get the two to mesh.

25 What point does the writer make about children?

   A   They have no real need for formal learning.
   B   They are able to create new forms of language.
   C   They are able to communicate in the absence of language.
   D   Their minds are sharper than we think.

26 What point is made about the process of learning to write?

   A   It is facilitated by machinery.
   B   It is best done collaboratively.
   C   It prepares us for other concepts.
   D   It requires a conscious effort.

Part 3

You are going to read an extract from a magazine article about global warming. Seven paragraphs have been removed from the extract. Choose from the paragraphs **A–H** the one which fits each gap (**27–33**). There is one extra paragraph which you do not need to use.

Mark your answers **on the separate answer sheet**.

The Heat is On

We've all heard of global warming, but just how much warmer will the earth get and how will it affect our lives?

Almost everyone has some idea of what global warming is all about, but no one is quite sure about its consequences. A warmer climate is likely to mean changes to the weather in all parts of the world. And since the atmosphere is intimately linked to every aspect of the planet on which we live, any changes to climate will have significant knock-on effects for plants and animals, as well as water and soils.

27

There is no doubt, for example, that over the last 100 years or so, human action has significantly increased the atmospheric concentrations of several gases – the so-called greenhouse gases – which are closely related to global temperature. It seems likely that these increased concentrations, which are set to continue building up in the near future, are already affecting global climate, but our poor knowledge and understanding of the global heat balance make the current and future situations uncertain. What we do know is that atmospheric concentrations of greenhouse gases have fluctuated in close harmony with global temperatures over the past 40,000 years.

28

A lot of research has gone into predicting the conditions that will result from higher global temperatures. Most of this research uses computer programs known as general circulation models, or GCMs. They run on powerful computers, use fundamental laws of physics and chemistry to analyse the interaction of temperature, pressure, solar radiation and other climatic factors to predict climatic conditions for the past, present or future.

29

Despite these research difficulties, most people agree on perhaps the most important aspect of climatic change from the viewpoint of contemporary human societies: the rate of change will be faster than anything we have previously experienced. In this case, the approximate predictions produced by the GCMs are being used to gain some insight into the nature and conditions of the world that we will inhabit over the next few generations.

30

These forecasts should leave us in little doubt about the potential impact of climatic change on the natural environment and humans. Changes in climate have the potential to affect the geographical location of ecological systems, such as forests and grasslands, the mix of species they contain and their ability to provide the various benefits on which societies depend for their continued existence. Thus, the whole range of resources on which we rely is sensitive to changes in climate. This includes food production, water resources and human settlements. The effects, some of which are potentially irreversible, are likely to be unfavourable in many areas.

31

The most important climatic factor observed in this case was the rise, in recent decades, of the minimum temperature. Among other things, the warmer temperatures have meant fewer frosts, and this has caused less damage to harvests.

However, many of the predicted effects of future climate warming are far from beneficial. Relatively small changes in climate can influence the availability of water, either due to long-term drying of the climate or by increasing the frequency of droughts. Associated problems are likely to arise first in arid and semi-arid

regions and more humid areas where demand or pollution have already created shortages.

32	

A further undesirable effect is likely to be changes to glacial processes. This will impact on glacier ice, ground ice and sea ice, which in turn will affect vegetation, wildlife habitats and human structures and facilities. Indeed, there is a strong possibility that the Arctic's ice cover will melt completely, making marine transport and oil and gas exploration easier but increasing the danger from icebergs.

But probably the most dramatic and visible effect of global warming in the twenty-first or 'greenhouse' century will be the rise in sea levels. This will be caused by the thermal expansion of the oceans – warmer water occupies a greater volume than cold water – and the added input from melting ice. With scientists calculating that about half of the world's population live in coastal zones, the consequences of rising sea levels are potentially very severe.

33	

Arguably the most severe consequences would be experienced by several small, low-lying island states, since entire countries could cease to exist if worst-case scenarios are realised. The consequences would be devastating, not only for the people and culture of these islands, but also for the countries that would need to accommodate those who had been displaced.

A The Mediterranean Basin is one example of this and in recent decades decreasing trends in precipitation totals have already been identified in western-central parts of the basin as well as marked changes in seasonality. A clear tendency for rainfall to be concentrated into a shorter period of the year has been noted in the Alentejo region of southern Portugal, with the proportion of annual rainfall falling in autumn and winter, increasing at the expense of spring totals.

B Unfortunately, they are simplifications of the real world and have numerous deficiencies. Their results are only approximate and they are also slow to run and expensive to use. Part of the problem is that we do not understand fully all the processes of the climatic system, although we do realise its complexity.

C Increased flooding and inundation are the most obvious results, with London, New York and Tokyo being just a few of the candidates for significant disruption. Huge numbers of people stand to lose their homes and livelihoods and this could produce many millions of environmental refugees.

D But this would not be true for all. In fact, some climate change impacts will probably be beneficial. Scientists in some countries have already identified useful environmental trends that are closely linked to the warming that has occurred to date. In Australia, for example, research has shown that the average yield of wheat has increased by about 0.5 tonnes per hectare since 1952, and climate trends have played a significant part in this greater food production.

E This would indicate that the two are almost certainly related. Evidence gleaned from a range of sources suggests that our planet has warmed at the surface by about 6°C over the past century. Most scientists think that this trend is unlikely to be natural in origin and is, in part, a result of human pollution of the atmosphere.

F This proves that the earth's climate has never been static and human impact on climate has been relatively minor, compared to naturally occurring large-scale perturbations. Ice ages, for example, result from natural changes in the earth's orbit around the sun. But the most worrying type of human-induced climatic change has been brought about through modifications to the natural atmospheric mix of greenhouse gases.

G We humans have learned to use such natural resources to our advantage, enabling us to produce food, build great cities and support six billion members of the human race. Any changes to these resources have to be taken seriously. The problem we have is knowing just how the world will change, and what is causing these changes.

H Currently, they suggest that the average annual global surface temperature will increase by between 1°C and 3.5°C by the year 2100; that the average sea level around the world will rise by 15–95 cm; and that changes in the spatial and temporal patterns of precipitation will occur. Scientists also expect extreme weather conditions, such as heatwaves, floods and droughts, to become more frequent in some places.

Part 4

You are going to read an article on maps. For questions **34–40**, choose the answer (**A**, **B**, **C** or **D**) which you think fits best according to the text.

Mark your answers **on the separate answer sheet**.

Maps

The purpose of a map is to express graphically the relations of points and features on the earth's surface to each other. These are determined by distance and direction. In early times distance was often expressed in units of time, for example 'so many hours' march' or 'a day's journey by river', but such measurements gave more information about the relative ease of crossing the local terrain than they did about actual distance. The other element is direction, but for the ordinary traveller, whose main concern was 'Where do I go from here?' and 'How far away is it?', the accurate representation of direction was not of primary importance. Partly for this reason, written itineraries for a long time rivalled maps. Even today, certain types of maps, for example those showing railway systems, may make little attempt to show true directions. Similarly, conspicuous landmarks along a route were at first indicated by signs, realistic or conventional, and varied in size to indicate their importance. Clearly the conventions employed varied with the purpose of the map, and also from place to place, so that in studying early maps the first essential is to understand the particular convention employed.

The history of cartography is largely that of the increase in the accuracy with which these elements of distance and direction are determined and in the comprehensiveness of the map content. In this development, cartography has called in other sciences to its aid. For example, instead of determining direction by observing the position of a shadow at midday, or of a constellation in the night sky, or even of a steady wind, use was made of terrestrial magnetism through the magnetic compass, and instruments were evolved which enabled horizontal angles to be calculated with great accuracy.

The application of astronomical concepts, and the extension of the knowledge of the world through exploration, encouraged attempts to map the known world. Then astronomers discovered that the earth is not a perfect sphere, but is flattened slightly at the poles, which introduced further refinements into the mapping of large areas. Meanwhile, the demands being made of the map maker were shifting significantly. The traveller or the merchant ceased to be the sole user of maps. The soldier, especially after the introduction of artillery, and the problems of range, field of fire, and dead ground which it raised, demanded an accurate representation of the surface features, in place of the earlier conventional or pictorial delineation, and a solution in any degree satisfactory was not reached until the contour was invented.

Then there was the archaeologist, the historian and, much later, the modern geographer, each with their own special requirements. In order to address these, the present-day cartographer has had to evolve methods of mapping all kinds of 'distributions', from geological strata and climatic regimes to land use. It is the present widespread recognition of the value of the map in the co-ordination and interpretation of phenomena in many sciences that has led to what may truly be called a modern renaissance of cartography.

It would be misleading of me to represent the stages summarily sketched above as being either continuous or consecutive. There have been periods of retrogression or stagnation, broken by others of rapid development, during which outmoded ideas have held their place beside the new. Again, cartographers have constantly realised the theoretical basis for progress, but have had to wait for technical improvement in their instruments before they could apply their new ideas. Since the easiest way to make a map is to copy an old one, and considerable capital has often been locked up in printing plates or stock, map publishers have often been resistant to new ideas. Consequently, maps must never be accepted uncritically as evidence of contemporary knowledge and technique.

Clearly, the maps, many thousands in number, which have come down to us today, are the results of much human work and thought. They constitute therefore an invaluable record for the student of man's past. It is above all this aspect that makes the study of historical cartography so fascinating and so instructive.

34 Why might early maps have been misleading?

    A   Distances could not be calculated reliably.
    B   They were based on written itineraries.
    C   They were drawn by ordinary travellers.
    D   Distances tended to be exaggerated.

35 What problem did early maps exhibit when showing landmarks?

    A   The signs used bore little relation to the landmarks.
    B   The selection of landmarks was flawed.
    C   They used symbols that were not standardised.
    D   They sometimes incorporated unimportant features.

36 In the second paragraph, the writer says that better quality map-making was facilitated by

    A   a greater understanding of climatic factors.
    B   greater accuracy in draughtsmanship.
    C   more precision in measurement.
    D   more intensive map production.

37 What prompted the search for a more precise means of mapping the physical geography of the landscape?

    A   a discovery in astronomy
    B   the growth of mathematical science
    C   the activities of the great explorers
    D   military considerations

38 The writer implies that present-day cartographers

    A   have to be highly adaptable.
    B   enjoy a high status in the scientific world.
    C   are rediscovering the value of early maps.
    D   have achieved something extraordinary.

39 The writer points out that his own account of the history of map-making is based on

    A   a rather traditional view.
    B   certain theoretical assumptions.
    C   a simplification of complex processes.
    D   somewhat unreliable data.

40 What point is the writer making about publishers of maps?

    A   Their technical equipment holds them back.
    B   They are inhibited by financial considerations.
    C   They are critical of cartographers.
    D   Their conservatism limits map production.

PAPER 2   WRITING (2 hours)

Part 1

You **must** answer this question. Write your answer in **300–350** words in an appropriate style.

---

1 Your tutor shows you two extracts from articles about employment in the future.

> The rise in unemployment cannot be stopped. The number of unemployed people will continue to rise as more and more jobs are done by machines and computers. We now live in a global economy, and more and more people will lose their jobs as competition and profits dominate the world.

> **The future offers all kinds of exciting job opportunities. New kinds of industry are developing all the time, and there will always be new kinds of employment. The future of work has never looked better.**

Your tutor asks you to write an essay about employment in the future, responding to the points raised and giving your own views on the matter.

Write your **essay**.

Visual materials for Paper 5

TEST 1 PAPER 5   Conference programme – Pressure at work

1A

1B

1C

1D

1E

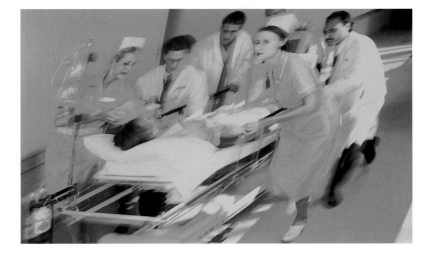

1F

1G

2A

2B

2C

2D

2E

2F

2G

3A

3B

3C

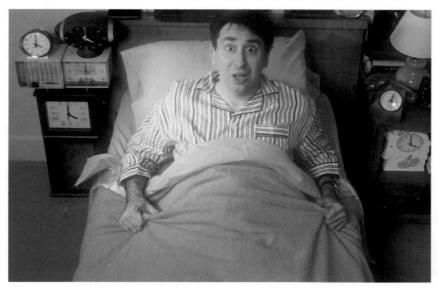

3D

3E

3F

4A

4B

4C

4D

4E

TEST 1

In what ways can we best understand the history of our country?

- books
- people
- places

TEST 2

What are the effects of technological development on our lives?

- work
- health
- leisure

TEST 3

What makes someone a good learner?

- different ages
- interest
- role of teacher

TEST 4

What does successful communication between people depend on?

- circumstances
- relationships
- use of language

TEST 1

Why do many older people say that the past was better?

- education
- social values
- pace of life

TEST 2

What makes a language develop and change?

- different uses
- different generations
- different fashions

TEST 3

What are the attractions and drawbacks of being a teacher?

- working with people
- working conditions
- sharing knowledge

TEST 4

How has technology helped, or not helped, communication?

- convenience
- dependence
- cost

TEST 4

What are the strengths and weaknesses of the different forms of mass media?

- news
- education
- entertainment

Part 2

Write an answer to **one** of the questions **2–5** in this part. Write your answer in **300–350** words in an appropriate style.

---

2   A company is planning to launch a new magazine called *Healthy Lifestyles for the Young*. The editor wants to find out what people would like to read in the magazine, and is inviting proposals about the possible content as well as ideas on how to make the magazine appeal to young people.

Write a **proposal**.

3   A magazine called *Nature and Wild Life* is inviting readers to send in their ideas on helping to protect endangered animals, birds and plants. You decide to write a letter to the magazine with your suggestions.

Write your **letter**. Do not write any postal addresses.

4   A popular magazine has invited readers to send in articles for their series on 'Good Neighbours'. Readers are invited to write an article entitled 'Good neighbours are worth their weight in gold'. Write your article describing a particular occasion when a neighbour helped you out in a difficult situation, and say what you think makes a good neighbour.

Write your **article**.

5   Based on your reading of **one** of these books, write on **one** of the following.

(a) Anne Tyler: *The Accidental Tourist*

A magazine is inviting readers to send in articles on the theme of marital breakdown in modern literature. You write an article in which you discuss the reasons for the failure of Sarah and Macon's marriage in *The Accidental Tourist*, and say how far you agree or disagree with Macon's comment that it was due to 'essential incompatibility'.

Write your **article**.

(b) John Wyndham: *The Day of the Triffids*

You read the following in a letter to a literary magazine:

> *In science fiction the humans are always represented as being better than any other life-forms they meet.*

Having just read *The Day of the Triffids*, you decide to write a letter to the editor saying whether you agree or disagree with this statement, making reference to the human characters and the triffids in the story.

Write your **letter**. Do not write any postal addresses.

(c) Graham Greene: *Our Man in Havana*

The Arts Section of a newspaper is planning a series of reviews on famous spy stories. You decide to send in a review of *Our Man in Havana*, focusing on Wormold as a secret agent and showing how far the novel can be regarded as a typical spy story.

Write your **review**.

PAPER 3   USE OF ENGLISH (1 hour 30 minutes)

Part 1

For questions **1–15**, read the text below and think of the word which best fits each space. Use only **one** word in each space. There is an example at the beginning **(0)**.

Write your answers in CAPITAL LETTERS **on the separate answer sheet**.

Example: | 0 | A | | | | | | | | | | | | | | | | | | | | |

Water on the moon

As **(0)** ......*a*....... result of the recent discovery of lunar water, the moon has suddenly become a far more interesting place for investors, **(1)** .... must now view the long-term prospects with optimism. The last manned mission to the moon drew **(2)** .... a close in 1973, **(3)** .... two astronauts from *Apollo 17* climbed back into their lunar module, **(4)** .... collected a lot of moonrock, but bereft **(5)** .... any future plans. Now the moon shines brighter for astronauts and scientists alike, **(6)** .... to the existence of **(7)** .... might be billions of tonnes of water at **(8)** .... poles.

There is **(9)** .... high-tech substitute for water in space exploration. To support the international space station, **(10)** .... has cost at least $100,000 a day to send water **(11)** .... orbit. Not **(12)** .... would lunar water cut these costs, but it would additionally be used for rocket fuel, **(13)** .... two components, liquid hydrogen and liquid oxygen, are the elements found in water.

Scientists are particularly excited **(14)** .... , given the absence of an atmosphere, lunar water has never been recycled and they believe, therefore, that it **(15)** .... very well hold clues to the formation of the solar system itself.

Part 2

For questions **16–25**, read the text below. Use the word given in capitals at the end of some of the lines to form a word that fits in the space in the same line. There is an example at the beginning **(0)**.

Write your answers in CAPITAL LETTERS **on the separate answer sheet**.

Example: | 0 | C | H | A | L | L | E | N | G | I | N | G | | | | | | | | |

ANTHROPOLOGY

One of the most **(0)** ...challenging... aspects of the science of anthropology   **CHALLENGE**

comes from its fieldwork. Certainly, in its **(16)** .... as a profession,   **INFANT**

anthropology was distinguished by its concentration on so-called 'primitive

societies' in which social **(17)** .... appeared to be fairly limited and social   **INSTITUTE**

interaction to be conducted almost **(18)** .... face-to-face. Such societies,   **EXCLUDE**

it was felt, provided anthropologists with a valuable **(19)** .... into the   **SEE**

workings of society that contrasted with the many complexities of more highly

developed societies. There was also a sense that the ways of life represented

by these smaller societies were rapidly **(20)** .... and that preserving a   **APPEAR**

record of them was a matter of some urgency.

The **(21)** .... of anthropologists to the first-hand collection of data led them   **COMMIT**

to some of the most **(22)** .... places on earth. Most often they worked   **ACCESS**

alone. Such lack of contact with other people created feelings of intense

(23) .... in some anthropologists, especially in the early stages of   **LONELY**

fieldwork. Nevertheless, this process of **(24)** .... in a totally alien culture   **IMMERSE**

continues to attract men and women to anthropology, and is

(25) .... the most effective way of understanding in depth how other   **DENY**

people see the world.

71

Part 3

For questions **26–31**, think of **one** word only which can be used appropriately in all three sentences. Here is an example (**0**).

Example:

0 Some of the tourists are hoping to get compensation for the poor state of the hotel, and I think they have a very .... case.

There's no point in trying to wade across the river, the current is far too ....

If you're asking me which of the candidates should get the job, I'm afraid I don't have any .... views either way.

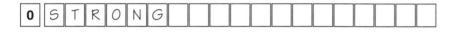

Write **only** the missing word in CAPITAL LETTERS **on the separate answer sheet**.

---

26 After further .... , the company decided not to appeal against the council's refusal of their planning application.

The fact that we have not asked you to do this job is no .... on your work.

For a moment everyone in the room was dazzled by the .... of the sun on the glass.

27 Stuart is an excellent actor but he cannot .... criticism of any sort.

The insurers said the company would have to .... some of the costs of repairing the damaged wall.

Both of the children .... a very strong resemblance to their grandfather.

28 Children can be very difficult at the age of two, but it's just a developmental .... they go through.

Negotiations between the two companies are at a crucial .... and a decision is expected later today.

The mayor's opening speech set the .... for the programme of events to celebrate the village's 800th anniversary.

29   The interpretation given is, in fact, the .... taken by most modern thinkers.

Kate could hear the sighs of impatience growing in the .... of customers behind her.

The company's annual trading figures remained broadly in .... with expectations.

30   Dr Saunders was completely overwhelmed by the .... of work she faced every day.

If you turn the .... up any more, we'll get complaints from the neighbours.

The writer's second .... of short stories has been well received by critics, though sales are disappointing.

31   Everybody who read the articles must have been .... by the courage shown by the little boy in the face of such adversity.

Mr and Mrs Davenport bought a house in France a few years ago and ....
there once they had retired.

It was clear from the graceful way in which the girl .... that she had had ballet training.

Part 4

For questions **32–39**, complete the second sentence so that it has a similar meaning to the first sentence, using the word given. **Do not change the word given.** You must use between **three** and **eight** words, including the word given.

Here is an example **(0)**.

Example:

0 Do you mind if I watch while you paint?

objection

Do you .... you while you paint?

| **0** | *have any objection to my watching* |

Write **only** the missing words **on the separate answer sheet**.

---

32 The news of the merger came as a complete surprise to the workers.

aback

The workers .... the news of the merger.

33 Everybody in the audience stood to applaud the actor's performance.

standing

The actor was .... for his performance.

34 Do phone us when you arrive at the airport, even if it is late.

how

No .... is when you arrive at the airport, do phone us.

35 It was obvious that Andrew was completely unaware of what was happening.

idea

Andrew obviously had .... on.

36 I seem to have been in this queue for hours.

joined

It seems like .... this queue.

37 Would it be possible to speak to you in private for a moment?

having

Is there .... word with you?

38 There is a remarkable similarity in how the two sisters dress.

alike

The two sisters .... way they dress.

39 What explanation can we offer for this sudden drop in temperature?

account

How .... temperature has suddenly
dropped?

Part 5

For questions **40–44**, read the following texts on psychology. For questions **40–43**, write a word or short phrase. You do not need to write complete sentences. For question **44**, write a summary according to the instructions given.

Write your answers to questions **40–44 on the separate answer sheet**.

On the one hand, the psychology of perception is connected to the senses themselves (sight, hearing, etc.), and on the other hand to the sensory data received. The constancy and repetitiveness of stimuli, the way they are represented and their reciprocal relationships are perceived to different degrees by the sensory organs. Each individual learns about the world through these organs, but what we discern not only depends on our previous experiences, but also on our needs.

The things around us create spheres of stimuli to which we react as a whole, often without considering the component parts. For example, we perceive a picture or a melody, not flecks of colour or individual notes. Similarly, we place our experiences within a framework of time and space, so it is natural for us to accept the cause-and-effect relationship between our pressing a switch and a light coming on. Perceptual identification develops in a child precisely through this constancy and repetition of events, which is responsible for our awareness of the permanent qualities and functions of individual objects.

We acquire our perception of the world intellectually. Hence when we turn our attention from one thing to another, we believe that what we are looking at stays where it is, or if it is moving, that it continues to move; in other words that the object 'behaves' as we think it should.

40 What, according to the writer, do people do with the sensory data they receive?

....

41 Explain in your own words how children learn to recognise things in the world.

....

Our awareness of the material world requires physical receptors, the five senses which enable us to see, hear, feel, taste and smell. These reveal our environment to us, but only those selected aspects of it in relation to which we have to act and react. For in selecting, our senses exclude much more than they let in. They have developed to aid our survival as organisms occupying our particular evolutionary niche, and they accordingly function as meshes through   **line 6** which only a certain range of signals can pass. If the whole range of light waves affected us, we would be unable to distinguish objects affecting our survival. If every sound wave registered in our consciousness, we would be so confused by the universal cacophony as to be unable to react to the sounds that we need to hear.

The process by which we are aware of the physical environment is extremely complex. It is also normally a successful process as otherwise the species would not have survived. Each species has been programmed through the evolutionary process to interpret the signals of the physical environment correctly as they affect that particular life form, and this applies to humans too. There are of course some cultural differences, although these do not affect the basic fact that we have very little cognitive freedom at this level of awareness.

42 Explain why the writer says that the senses are like 'meshes' (line 6).

....

43 How do human beings in different parts of the world interpret the signals of their physical environment?

....

44 In a paragraph of **50–70** words, summarise **in your own words as far as possible** what the two texts say would be the effect on our lives if our senses allowed us to be fully aware of all the stimuli from the physical world. Write your summary **on the separate answer sheet**.

PAPER 4 LISTENING (40 minutes approximately)

Part 1

You will hear four different extracts. For questions **1–8**, choose the answer (**A**, **B** or **C**) which fits best according to what you hear. There are two questions for each extract.

Extract 1

You hear part of an interview with a balloonist talking about his career.

1 What impression does the interviewer gain from reading the balloonist's book?

    A He aimed to become rich.
    B He was only interested in having fun.
    C He has turned a fantasy into reality.

1

2 How did the balloonist respond to his first balloon flight?

    A He felt privileged to have had this opportunity.
    B He used it as a springboard to get into advertising.
    C He saw the potential to exploit ballooning commercially.

2

Extract 2

You hear part of an interview with a photographer about his new book of photographs of famous women.

3 What was the photographer's aim in producing the book?

    A to promote only high-profile celebrities
    B to show a hidden facet of the women
    C to explore contradictions in the women's personalities

3

4 What was the particular challenge of each photograph?

    A changing the popular image of the famous women
    B capturing the essence of the women's fame
    C dealing with information given in confidence

Extract 3

You hear a football fan talking about his team on a radio phone-in programme.

5 In the speaker's opinion, the football team lost their recent match because of

  A the players' lack of enthusiasm.
  B insufficient training for the team.
  C a poor managerial decision.

6 Why is the speaker cautiously optimistic about the team's future?

  A He is sure that the team can be rebuilt.
  B He knows who the new goal-scorer will be.
  C He is confident that the fans will support their team.

Extract 4

You hear a museum curator talking on the radio about a sail that was last used on a sailing ship about two hundred years ago.

7 What happened when the sail was put on show in the museum?

  A The museum had to re-organise its exhibition space.
  B The curator's factual research was appreciated by the public.
  C The exhibition had a more powerful effect than the curator had expected.

8 The curator describes the physical condition of the sail in order to stress its

  A fragility.
  B authenticity.
  C beauty.

Part 2

You will hear a short talk about a bird of prey called the kestrel. For questions **9–17**, complete the sentences with a word or short phrase.

The name 'kestrel' derives from its cry which sounds like a

	9

Originally, kestrels only used

	10

as breeding sites.

In urban areas, kestrels are often to be found on the

	11

of buildings.

The kestrel is able to

	12

rapidly and this has ensured its survival until now.

Sheep eat vegetation and this destroys the

	13

needed by the kestrels' prey.

Problems with

	14

are caused by prolonged rain and snow.

The current adult kestrel population is believed to number

	15

thousand birds.

Relatively few young kestrels survive because of

	16

by their parents.

Information about the

	17

of kestrels is the most important fact to include on the sighting form.

Part 3

You will hear the historian, George Davies, talking about society and the theatre in England in the time of William Shakespeare. For questions **18–22**, choose the answer (**A**, **B**, **C** or **D**) which fits best according to what you hear.

---

18   What is Professor Davies' view of the level of literacy in sixteenth-century England?

    A   It was increasing steadily.
    B   It matched his expectations.
    C   It contributed to social unrest.
    D   It was uniform across the social spectrum.

	18

19   What, according to Professor Davies, was the advantage of the usual method of communication in the sixteenth century?

    A   People were more direct in the way they spoke.
    B   It made people patient listeners.
    C   People absorbed more of what they heard.
    D   It encouraged close relationships between people.

	19

20   Professor Davies believes that Shakespeare's company developed their basic acting skills by

    A   reciting their lessons.
    B   attending special voice classes.
    C   learning from Shakespeare himself.
    D   imitating the style of other actors.

	20

21   What, in Professor Davies' view, was the advantage of sixteenth-century theatres?

    A   They made use of natural light.
    B   They were shaped like a sports arena.
    C   They encouraged the appreciation of drama.
    D   The performances were complemented by everyday life.

	21

22   According to Professor Davies, sixteenth-century plays were expected to deal with

    A   personal confessions.
    B   character development.
    C   intimate emotions.
    D   matters of state.

	22

Part 4

You will hear a conversation in which Clare and Tom, who teach English to foreign students at the same language school, discuss Tom's first week at the school. For questions **23–28**, decide whether the opinions are expressed by only one of the speakers, or whether the speakers agree.

Write **C** for Clare,
         T for Tom,
or   **B** for Both, where they agree.

---

23 The physical conditions don't live up to the image the school wants to promote.

> 23

24 The owners of the school need to adapt to cope with the realities of competition.

> 24

25 Schools can stay independent if they target specific groups of customers.

> 25

26 Professionally, teachers benefit more from working with colleagues in the same field than with those in different fields.

> 26

27 Teachers are responsible for managing their relationships with classes.

> 27

28 Job satisfaction is more important than the salary.

> 28

PAPER 5   SPEAKING (19 minutes)

There are two examiners. One (the Interlocutor) conducts the test, providing you with the necessary materials and explaining what you have to do. The other examiner (the Assessor) will be introduced to you, but then takes no further part in the interaction.

Part 1 (3 minutes)

The Interlocutor first asks you and your partner a few questions which focus on information about yourselves and personal opinions.

Part 2 (4 minutes)

In this part of the test you and your partner are asked to talk together. The Interlocutor places a set of pictures on the table in front of you. This stimulus provides the basis for a discussion. The Interlocutor first asks an introductory question which focuses on one or two of the pictures. After about a minute, the Interlocutor gives you both a decision-making task based on the same set of pictures.

The pictures for Part 2 are on pages C6–C7 of the colour section.

Part 3 (12 minutes)

You are each given the opportunity to talk for two minutes, to comment after your partner has spoken and to take part in a more general discussion.

The Interlocutor gives you a card with a question written on it and asks you to talk about it for two minutes. After you have spoken, your partner is first asked to comment and then the Interlocutor asks you both another question related to the topic on the card. This procedure is repeated, so that your partner receives a card and speaks for two minutes, you are given an opportunity to comment and a follow-up question is asked.

Finally, the Interlocutor asks some further questions, which leads to a discussion on a general theme related to the subjects already covered in Part 3.

The cards for Part 3 are on pages C10–C11 of the colour section.

Test 4

PAPER 1   READING (1 hour 30 minutes)

Part 1

For questions **1–18**, read the three texts below and decide which answer (**A**, **B**, **C** or **D**) best fits each gap.

Mark your answers **on the separate answer sheet**.

Surviving in a Foreign Land

I have been welcomed warmly. It's a sociable and well-provisioned base camp in a very, very isolated place. At any one time, there are some forty odd souls – scientists, students, weathermen, satellite trackers – in a **(1)** .... community where everyone mucks **(2)** .... . My school French is proving adequate – just – to **(3)** .... , but not to chat or banter. I miss the nuances, and my phrasebook is useless at breakfast.

There is no practical problem for me in this, but initially there was a problem of self-confidence. I found myself slightly dreading mealtimes. I would **(4)** .... , worried about which table to choose, terrified at the silence which **(5)** .... when I spoke, anxious in a way I cannot remember since the first weeks of school. I still grin inanely, or panic when people talk to me. I suspect the cause of this occasional depression is nothing to do with loss of company or communication; it's because I've lost the social predominance which my own gift of the gab has always **(6)** .... me.

1	**A**	close-knit	**B**	close-fitting	**C**	close-run	**D**	close-cropped
2	**A**	about	**B**	around	**C**	in	**D**	up
3	**A**	articulate	**B**	communicate	**C**	converse	**D**	interpret
4	**A**	bend back	**B**	turn back	**C**	lean back	**D**	hang back
5	**A**	dropped	**B**	fell	**C**	hit	**D**	struck
6	**A**	afforded	**B**	empowered	**C**	entitled	**D**	presented

Elliot

When I first met Elliot, I was just a young author like any other and he took no notice of me. He never forgot a face though, and when I **(7)** .... him here or there he shook hands with me cordially, but showed no desire to **(8)** .... our acquaintance; and if I saw him at the opera, say, he being with a person of high rank, he was **(9)** .... not to catch sight of me. But then I **(10)** .... to make a somewhat startling success as a playwright, and presently I became aware that Elliot **(11)** .... me with a warmer feeling. One day, I received a note from him asking me to lunch and I conceived the **(12)** .... that he was trying me out. But from then on, since my success had brought me many new friends, I began to see him more frequently.

7	**A**	ran across	**B**	fell in with	**C**	saw through	**D**	took up with
8	**A**	accelerate	**B**	advance	**C**	further	**D**	promote
9	**A**	inclined	**B**	inspired	**C**	vulnerable	**D**	susceptible
10	**A**	developed	**B**	happened	**C**	transpired	**D**	grew
11	**A**	held	**B**	observed	**C**	took	**D**	regarded
12	**A**	impression	**B**	suspicion	**C**	notion	**D**	opinion

Alfred Hitchcock

The film director Alfred Hitchcock always insisted that he didn't care about the **(13)** .... matter of his films, or **(14)** .... about the acting, but that he did care about the photography and the soundtrack and all the technical ingredients. For Hitchcock, it wasn't a message that **(15)** .... the audience, nor was it a great performance; he believed that people are aroused by pure film, **(16)** .... of their cultural background. Therefore, if a picture is designed correctly, in terms of its emotional **(17)** .... , the Japanese audience should scream at the same moment as the Indian audience.

Hitchcock's self-appraisal was always precise, rational, deceptively unanswerable; he was a man of reason and a craftsman of genius who liked to hear an audience scream. He didn't deal in speculation, abstraction or intellectual allusion, and his assessment of his own screen characters was not exploratory. He set his **(18)** .... on film, pure film, and the most dispassionate, mathematically calculable beauty of what a strip of film can be made to do to an audience.

13	**A**	topic	**B**	content	**C**	subject	**D**	theme
14	**A**	whether	**B**	indeed	**C**	instead	**D**	rather
15	**A**	stirred	**B**	riled	**C**	raised	**D**	sparked
16	**A**	unremarked	**B**	unrelated	**C**	irrelevant	**D**	irrespective
17	**A**	involvement	**B**	feedback	**C**	impact	**D**	response
18	**A**	views	**B**	targets	**C**	aims	**D**	sights

Part 2

You are going to read four extracts which are all concerned in some way with academic disciplines. For questions **19–26**, choose the answer (**A**, **B**, **C** or **D**) which you think fits best according to the text.

Mark your answers **on the separate answer sheet**.

Oral History

The growing trend for historians to rely on oral evidence is not without its problems. It is naive to suppose that someone's testimony represents a pure distillation of past experience, for in an interview each party is affected by the other. It is the historian who selects the informant and indicates the area of interest; and even if he or she asks no questions and merely listens, the presence of an outsider affects the atmosphere in which the informant recalls the past and talks about it. The end product is conditioned both by the historian's social position *vis-à-vis* the informant, and by the terms in which he or she has learnt to analyse the past and which may well be communicated to the informant. In other words, historians must accept responsibility for their share in creating new evidence. But the difficulties are far from over when the historian is removed from the scene. For not even the informant is in direct touch with the past. His or her memories may be contaminated by what has been absorbed from other sources (especially the media); they may be overlaid by nostalgia ('times were good then'), or distorted by a sense of grievance about deprivation in childhood, which only took root in later life. To anyone listening, the feelings and attitudes are often what lends conviction to the testimony, yet they may be the emotional residue of later events rather than the period in question.

19 The writer thinks that historians who are collecting data from oral sources should

    A use methods of collecting the data that are demonstrably reliable.
    B adapt the way they conduct the interview to suit individual informants.
    C consider the extent to which they determine an informant's recollections.
    D avoid any bias they have in relation to the historical period being investigated.

20 What does the writer suggest about informants?

    A They may consciously be trying to please the historian.
    B Their objectivity is affected by a lack of historical perspective.
    C They select positive memories to form the basis of their accounts.
    D Their perceptions of the past are coloured by subsequent experiences.

Animal Science

There are two main approaches to animal science – the physiological and the 'whole animal'. Physiologists are mainly interested in how the body works, that is, in how the nerves, muscles and sense organs are coordinated to produce complex behaviour. Those taking the 'whole animal' approach, although they are often interested in the mechanisms of behaviour, study the behaviour of the intact animal and the factors that affect it.

Within the 'whole animal' approach, a distinction is often made between psychologists and ethologists. Psychologists have traditionally worked in laboratories on the learning abilities of a restricted range of species, mainly rats and pigeons. Ethologists have been more concerned with the naturally occurring, unlearnt behaviour of animals, often in their wild habitats. Although this distinction still exists to some extent, there is now a fruitful coming together of the two.

Among these types, it is the physiologists who like to emphasise that their methods are the more fundamental. However, even if we knew how every nerve cell operated in the performance of some pattern of behaviour, this would not remove the need for us to study it at a behavioural level also. Behaviour has its own organisation and its own units that we must use for its study. Trying to describe the nest-building behaviour of a bird in terms of the actions of individual nerve cells would be like trying to read a page of a book with a high-powered microscope.

21 What point does the writer make about ethologists and psychologists?

A They want to retain existing definitions of their specialisms.
B They have become equally cooperative.
C They each work with different species.
D They both study animals in the natural environment.

22 Through the example of the microscope, the writer implies that the physiological approach

A has too narrow a focus.
B over-emphasises behaviour.
C makes exaggerated claims about itself.
D ignores the way in which the nerve cells work.

The Social Sciences

A problem facing all students who come to study a social science for the first time is that they must do two things simultaneously. They must familiarise themselves with the substance or content of their new subject and, at the same time, they must learn the methodology of the subject. That is, they must become familiar not only with the knowledge and research findings which fill the textbooks but also with the methods by which the knowledge is obtained and organised, that is with the logical basis of the subject itself. The two elements are not separate; they are very closely related. Because we are all familiar with social life through our everyday experiences we may feel that the social sciences are very largely a matter of common-sense. But, as a look at any textbook will quickly indicate, though each of the social sciences is concerned with people in society, each discipline goes beyond common-sense understanding. Each discipline focuses on a particular aspect of social life, each uses particular methods of study and each employs its own set of concepts. It is this set of concepts, the most basic ideas in a subject, which constitutes the 'logical basis of the subject', which enables the social scientist to go beyond everyday common-sense and which distinguishes one discipline from another.

23   What point does the writer make about the social sciences?

   A   They are conceptual rather than practical subjects.
   B   They are more complex than may be imagined.
   C   They share a common set of research techniques.
   D   They are particularly accessible to the lay person.

24   In this paragraph the writer is

   A   introducing a subject.
   B   countering a criticism.
   C   defending his position.
   D   summing up his arguments.

Classical Architecture

To the classical world, that of Ancient Greece and Rome, architecture meant much more than the mere construction of buildings. 'Architecture', says the Roman architect Vitruvius, 'consists of Order, and of Arrangement, and of Proportion and Symmetry and Propriety and Distribution.' For several of these terms he gives a Greek equivalent: his definitions probably derived from an earlier Greek authority whose writings are lost to us. Utility and Function are not part of this definition, though in his book Vitruvius does go on to describe the best form and arrangements for different purposes of structure; but here, at the beginning, the aesthetic emphasis, architecture as an art, has priority. The origins of classical architecture are complex. There was obviously a long prehistory of basic construction, of hut habitations simple in form and material, both in Greece and Italy, which did not match up to Vitruvius' artistic requirements. Though these were, by definition, inartistic they nevertheless contributed an essential element of form, which persisted into the later sophisticated architectural concepts. However ornate it may appear from the outside, in essence the classical temple is a simple, single-roomed hut.

25 What does the writer suggest about Vitruvius?

   A   His primary concern was the ultimate uses of buildings.
   B   His thinking about art and architecture lacked originality.
   C   He set high aesthetic standards in buildings.
   D   He was more attracted to art than architecture.

26 What point is made about the classical temple in the final sentence?

   A   Its form derives from an earlier style of construction.
   B   It embodies an aesthetically pleasing architectural concept.
   C   Its external decoration detracts from its artistic merit.
   D   It is the highest achievement of Greek and Roman architecture.

Part 3

You are going to read a magazine article. Seven paragraphs have been removed from the article. Choose from the paragraphs **A–H** the one which fits each gap (**27–33**). There is one extra paragraph which you do not need to use.

Mark your answers **on the separate answer sheet**.

Music – The Challenge Ahead

Technological advances continue to transform our lives at work, at home and in our leisure activities. Susan Hallam discusses their impact on music in Britain.

In the latter part of the 20th century, we saw a rapid increase in the opportunities available for listening to music through radio, TV, records, tapes, CDs, videos and a rapidly developing range of multi-media techniques. Along with this, there has been a decline in the performance of live music and in the full-time employment opportunities for professional musicians.

27

Indeed, a society without music is surely unthinkable and it seems that the issue is not whether there will be music in the 21st century but what the nature of that music will be; and also whether there will be a continued perceived need for people to learn to play musical instruments.

28

In addition to its vocational significance, there is a growing body of evidence that playing an instrument may be beneficial to the development of skills at an earlier stage. Research in the USA has suggested that listening to or actively making music has a direct positive effect on spatial reasoning, one aspect of the measurement of intelligence.

29

Taking the idea behind such findings one step further, current research is investigating to what extent playing an instrument may even encourage the development of transferable skills. For instance, the need to practise regularly may assist in the acquisition of good study habits and focused concentration; playing in concerts may encourage habits of punctuality and good organisation.

30

While there are many possible scenarios, I believe that two possibilities are likely. Firstly, the kinds of music to which people will listen will become more diverse. New genres will develop which will integrate different styles. Secondly, there will be an increase in the use of technology to compose and perform music. This will widen access to composition as there will be less reliance on technical skill but at the same time, it is likely to further reduce the need for live performance and musicians whose role is solely related to it.

31

If this vision of the future is to be realised, what does the music profession need to do in preparation? The focus of instrumental tuition will need to change. Ways will need to be found to enable more people to learn to play a range of instruments, throughout their life span.

32

Crucial to the success of the process will be the training of musicians. They will need to be able to motivate, inspire and teach learners of all ages, develop skills for working with large and diverse groups and acquire the communication, social, entrepreneurial and management skills necessary for community work.

33

Finally, we need to strive towards raising the profile of music itself. Music plays a crucial role in our lives but all too often it is taken for granted. Those involved in the music profession at all levels need to work actively together to ensure that this changes.

A As a result, the impact on the instrumental curriculum and the measures used to assess progress through it will be such that they will need to adapt to maintain their relevance for a broader sector of the population. Ultimately, they will need to encompass a wider range of musical skills.

B For all these reasons, there is likely to be a continuing demand for instrumental teaching in the short term. What about the longer term picture? Is there likely to be a shift in focus and, if so, what direction will it take?

C I would respond to the latter question on a positive note. The music industry is one of the major generators of income in Britain and musical skill and talent will continue to be important in preparing individuals to work in a variety of professions, in particular those related to the media.

D This represents a fundamental change from traditional practice and it will be accompanied by the need to respond to demands for public accountability. Viewed positively, this should provide an opportunity for all those involved in music education to demonstrate the high quality of music tuition available.

E There seems little doubt that the widening access to music is likely to continue, fulfilling as it does so many human needs. On a national level, no major state occasion is without music. For individuals, it provides opportunities for numerous activities, formal and informal.

F One of the best-recognised functions is that of providing an outlet for emotional expression. Its influence on our moods can be therapeutic. It provides a means of communicating which goes beyond words and provides us with shared unspoken understandings.

G Developing in parallel with this trend is a likely increase in the number of people, across the whole age range, who wish to actively participate in music making. Such activities are likely to be community based and will reflect the musical traditions of that community whatever they may be.

H While these results are still to be successfully replicated, other data from Europe has indicated that an increase in group music lessons can have positive effects on social relationships in school and on concentration in young children and those with behavioural difficulties.

Part 4

You are going to read an extract from a novel. For questions **34–40**, choose the answer (**A**, **B**, **C** or **D**) which you think fits best according to the text.

Mark your answers **on the separate answer sheet**.

'You don't take sugar, do you?' shouted his secretary, not so much asking a question as stating a fact – as well she might, because she had been making Lancelot cups of coffee for many months. Her excuse for forgetting such things was that he wasn't normally supposed to be there. Actually nowadays he was usually there all the time, having discovered that to take up his proprietorial privilege of staying away was tantamount to opening the floodgates. Not for the first time he pondered the easy, imperceptibly divided stages by which he had progressed from valued counsellor, meeting authors and playwrights over lunch at carefully planned planning meetings complete with agenda, to hapless dogsbody moving one step ahead of catastrophe, with nowhere to park when he arrived at work in the mornings.

'This came,' she yelled, vaguely waving a manila folder before putting it down in front of him. 'From that chap in Los Angeles. You said you wanted to see it.' A typed label said: 'A World History of the Short, by Ian Cuthbert.' Just under that it said 'An Expanded Synopsis'. Lancelot did not want to see that word 'synopsis'. At the very least he wanted to see a label saying 'A First Draft'. Lancelot had already seen a synopsis of this book and did not really want to see another, however heavily revised. Ian Cuthbert had been given an advance of several thousands of pounds for this book during the initial flurry of activity when Lancelot had bought the firm. One of several old friends **line 18** from whom Lancelot had made the capital error of commissioning books, Ian Cuthbert **line 19** was a particularly flagrant proof that in such circumstances the possessor of a wayward **line 20** temperament, far from nerving himself to behave more predictably for friendship's **line 21** sake, will actually become less 'pindownable' than ever.

Lancelot skipped the blurb come preamble which he had read for what seemed like the hundredth time and sampled the synopsis proper. There was scarcely a phrase that he did not recognise at a glance. He closed the folder and shifted it to one side. Plainly at this rate Ian's manuscript would never be forthcoming. As well as almost wholly lacking the brilliance for which its author was supposed to be famous, the synopsis, under its doggedly frolicsome tone, had the unmistakable dead ring of a lost conviction. Lancelot remembered tales of a famous author-about-town whose last book, published incomplete after his death, had been coaxed from him chapter by chapter, one payment at a time. But in that case, the payments were fractions of a hypothetical advance which had never been given in the first place. Ian's advance had been enormous; a blatant reversal of the sound business principle by which authors must deliver a manuscript now in order to be paid with inflated currency later.

Lancelot, who had read modern languages at Oxford, could remember the day when Ian Cuthbert had been the most promising talent in a Cambridge so full of promise that it had made everywhere else feel provincial. Ian's contemporaries had plotted to take over the British theatre and in a remarkably short time they had actually done so. But their mental energy had seemed like indolence when you looked at Ian. He had worn his overcoat like a cape and talked about what one very famous French writer had said as if he had been there to overhear it. Yet for some reason, the whole frostily coruscating galaxy of Ian's creative intellect had remained locked in its closet. While less gifted deviants came out and conquered, Ian went further in. At the height of his influence as a literary taste-maker he was already notoriously difficult to deal with. Officially appointed by the relevant public agency to edit a comprehensive magazine of the arts, he was like a general with a million tons of equipment pinned down on the beach by nothing except an excess of opportunity. The magazine used up the budget for a dozen issues without appearing once. Similarly, his thrice-renewed three-year contract with one of the fashion magazines engendered little except legends about the size of his emolument, which was increased from generosity to extravagance in an attempt to make him produce more, and then from extravagance to munificence in an attempt to make him produce anything. At the editorial working breakfasts – there were always at least two of the titled photographers present to capture the scene for posterity – Ian spat witty venom through clenched teeth, and poured nitric acid on other people's ideas. Ten years later, he could scarcely be depended upon to turn up for his own funeral. Lancelot was on the verge of admitting to himself that 'A World History of the Short' had been a mistake from its inception.

34   What does the reader learn about Lancelot in the first paragraph?

   A   He regrets having delegated important work to his secretary.
   B   His business no longer runs as smoothly as it used to.
   C   He prefers entertaining clients to doing routine office work.
   D   His schedule is always tightly packed with appointments.

35   Which phrase, as it is used in the text, has a double meaning in the context of Lancelot's business initiatives?

   A   'flurry of activity' (line 18)
   B   'capital error' (line 19)
   C   'flagrant proof' (line 20)
   D   'wayward temperament' (lines 20–21)

36 According to the writer, how did Lancelot feel about Ian when he first commissioned him?

    A   He was aware that he was doing Ian a much-needed favour.

    B   He believed that his friendship with Ian would develop further.

    C   He suspected that he might have misjudged Ian's behaviour.

    D   He trusted that Ian would meet the requirements of the agreement.

37 How does Lancelot react to the 'synopsis' he has received from Ian?

    A   He is amazed to find that it contains no original thoughts or ideas.

    B   He has the impression that Ian is not taking the project seriously.

    C   He is convinced that Ian has other more pressing commitments.

    D   He realises that Ian's inflexibility restricts him to a certain writing style.

38 In recalling the story of another well-known author, Lancelot realises that

    A   money is not a motivating factor for people who are already famous.

    B   money can have a negative impact on relationships with others.

    C   he should have known better than to pay Ian when he did.

    D   he should have consulted others before making a deal with Ian.

39 What aspect of Ian's student days does Lancelot find hard to reconcile with his more recent experience of Ian?

    A   Ian's relationships with famous writers of that time

    B   the large number of Ian's peers who went into the theatre

    C   the fact that Ian outshone a highly talented peer group

    D   Ian's detachment from his artistic contemporaries

40 In comparing Ian's early career days to the experience of a general at war, the writer is suggesting that Ian

    A   might have benefited from a more restricted range of choices.

    B   might have done better in a different environment.

    C   was allowed to get away with too many misdemeanours.

    D   should have taken a more strategic approach to his work.

PAPER 2   WRITING (2 hours)

Part 1

You **must** answer this question. Write your answer in **300–350** words in an appropriate style.

---

1 Plans have been put forward to build a fast food restaurant in the historic centre of a town you know. Many local residents have expressed their disapproval:

> *'This means there will be even more traffic in the town!'*

> **'It will spoil the old-world character of the place.'**

> *'People come here to escape places like fast food restaurants, so many people will stop coming here.'*

However, you and other residents believe it will encourage more visitors to the town, increase revenue, and generate an interest in local history. You decide to send a proposal to the local council in which you say why you think the plans should be implemented.

Write your **proposal**.

Part 2

Write an answer to **one** of the questions **2–5** in this part. Write your answer in **300–350** words in an appropriate style.

---

2 You have recently returned from an adventure holiday with a group of students from your class, and you have been asked to write a review of your holiday for your college magazine. In your review, say why you would recommend it for a group of students who want a cheap but exciting holiday with opportunities for exploring interesting places, meeting different people, and experiencing a different lifestyle.

Write your **review**.

3 The Minister of Education is inviting people to send in proposals on various ways of improving education in their country. You decide to send in your ideas on the matter.

Write your **proposal**.

4 You read the following invitation in a magazine:

> Readers are invited to submit articles entitled 'I've always wanted to learn how to …'. Is there a skill that you have always wanted to learn? Write and tell us what your ambition is, what attracts you about this skill, and what you would do with this skill when you have learned it.

You decide to send in an article.

Write your **article**.

5 Based on your reading of **one** of these books, write on **one** of the following.

(a) Anne Tyler: *The Accidental Tourist*
A library is about to have an exhibition of books entitled 'Children in Twentieth Century Literature'. It has asked its readers for recommendations. Write a letter to the librarian recommending *The Accidental Tourist* as a possible book to appear in the exhibition. You should focus on Alexander and his relationship with his mother, Muriel, and with Macon.

Write your **letter**. Do not write any postal addresses.

(b) John Wyndham: *The Day of the Triffids*
The Drama Department of your college wants to make a video version of a story which is not only about dramatic events but also about human relationships. The producer has asked you to write a report on *The Day of the Triffids* in which you outline the dramatic events in the story, and describe their impact on the characters.

Write your **report**.

(c) Graham Greene: *Our Man in Havana*
A literary magazine is inviting readers to contribute articles on the way writers explore the relationship between different characters. You decide to write an article on *Our Man in Havana* showing how the relationship between Wormold and Dr Hasselbacher develops.

Write your **article**.

PAPER 3   USE OF ENGLISH (1 hour 30 minutes)

Part 1

For questions **1–15**, read the text below and think of the word which best fits each space. Use only **one** word in each space. There is an example at the beginning **(0)**.

Write your answers in CAPITAL LETTERS **on the separate answer sheet**.

Example: | 0 | W | H | E | N | | | | | | | | | | | | | |

History of music

Lovers of music who are a little rusty **(0)** ..when.. it comes to history shouldn't miss forthcoming issues of this magazine. In our most ambitious series of articles **(1)** .... date, we aim to span the history of western music in **(2)** .... entirety. Obviously, **(3)** .... the lack of space at our disposal, we cannot be totally comprehensive **(4)** .... we do feel we have a **(5)** .... than adequate overview of the socio-cultural context. If you're already feeling **(6)** .... off by the prospect of a rather dry history lesson, then I must stress how unlike a lesson these articles will be. **(7)** .... the extent to which you might be familiar **(8)** .... the historical background, you must read these articles for the insight they give **(9)** .... the music itself.

In **(10)** .... to this, the series will represent a guide for readers whose aim is to build an essential music collection. Now **(11)** .... this strike you **(12)** .... yet another voyage through familiar territory, then you may be in for some surprises, because our expert writers are nothing if **(13)** .... unpredictable. In view of the reputation of those involved, **(14)** .... thing is guaranteed – the music chosen to illustrate their histories will be **(15)** .... from run-of-the-mill.

Part 2

For questions **16–25**, read the text below. Use the word given in capitals at the end of some of the lines to form a word that fits in the space in the same line. There is an example at the beginning **(0)**.

Write your answers in CAPITAL LETTERS **on the separate answer sheet**.

Example: | 0 | U | N | D | E | R | G | O | N | E | | | | | | | | | | | |

The image of science

The image that we have of science has **(0)** ...undergone... radical change **GO**

in the last hundred years. An enormous **(16)** .... explosion, together with a **TECHNOLOGY**

number of very real **(17)** .... about the environment and all the moral and **ANXIOUS**

political ramifications of economic growth have **(18)** .... put science at the **QUESTION**

centre of public debate.

The twentieth century began with a challenge to the **(19)** .... that human **ASSUME**

knowledge was approaching completion. It will come, perhaps, as something

of a surprise to all of us to realise that the emergence of this highly **(20)** .... **DESTROY**

process came both from within and outside science.

New scientific theories **(21)** .... reveal the limitations of the old perspective. **OVERWHELM**

We had thought that the world, understood through the medium of rational

(22) .... , was, indeed, the real world. Now we know that this was no more **BE**

than a simplification that just happened to work. Once we realise this, though,

we can move in a number of opposing directions. We can re-evaluate all

knowledge **(23)** .... and decide that it is eternally fragmentary and full of a **PESSIMISM**

vast number of **(24)** .... , or we can be more positive and view these vast **PERFECTION**

explosions of scientific awareness as new challenges still to come and as

celebrations of the **(25)** .... that the human imagination has so far scaled. **HIGH**

Part 3

For questions **26–31**, think of **one** word only which can be used appropriately in all three sentences. Here is an example **(0)**.

Example:

0 Some of the tourists are hoping to get compensation for the poor state of the hotel, and I think they have a very .... case.

There's no point in trying to wade across the river, the current is far too ....

If you're asking me which of the candidates should get the job, I'm afraid I don't have any .... views either way.

Write **only** the missing word in CAPITAL LETTERS **on the separate answer sheet**.

---

26 His uncle's resignation .... the way for Tom to take over the business.

Susan .... a shelf to make room for the books she had recently bought.

As a result of new evidence produced in court today, Smith was .... of all blame.

27 The old house had been neglected and was in a deplorable ....

Until the 18ᵗʰ century, Scotland was an independent .... with its own system of government.

In many countries, the local authorities rather than the .... are responsible for maintaining roads, schools and hospitals.

28 I find it difficult to .... myself deadlines because I need some flexibility in my work.

My brother .... up a new business last year, and it's really taken off.

My favourite poem has been .... to music and sounds beautiful as a song.

29 Despite assurances from the tour company's local representatives, the stranded holidaymakers .... unconvinced by the reasons given for the cancellation of their flight.

Does anything .... of the castle's original furnishings, or have all these items been brought in from elsewhere?

Now that the farewell concert has taken place, only the group's financial affairs .... to be wound up.

30 Polly has .... an enormous amount in travelling expenses following her trip to the USA.

My boss has .... to be a direct descendant of the famous explorer.

The bank's collapse .... many victims in the city's financial institutions.

31 When she goes out too much, Samantha starts to .... behind with her homework.

The magazines on the market tend to .... into three main groups.

Following the opening of a rival nightclub, *Cinderella's* has begun to .... out of favour with the city's young people.

Part 4

For questions **32–39**, complete the second sentence so that it has a similar meaning to the first sentence, using the word given. **Do not change the word given**. You must use between **three** and **eight** words, including the word given.

Here is an example **(0)**.

Example:

0 Do you mind if I watch you while you paint?

objection

Do you .... you while you paint?

0	have any objection to my watching

Write **only** the missing words **on the separate answer sheet**.

---

32 Paul's son was driving the car when the accident happened.

time

The car was .... of the accident.

33 It was Nick's advice that saved me from bankruptcy.

it

Had .... have gone bankrupt.

34 The police never actually accused Thomas of committing a crime.

point

At .... Thomas of committing a crime.

35 Neither of these carpets is any better than the other.

choose

There's not .... these two carpets.

102

36 You are absolutely forbidden to smoke anywhere in the factory.

total

There .... anywhere in the factory.

37 Jenny doesn't mind whether she comes to London on either Monday or Tuesday.

no

It .... whether she comes to London on Monday or Tuesday.

38 Did the football team play any better last weekend?

in

Was there any .... last weekend?

39 In particular, the school library was criticised by the inspectors because of its poor lighting.

singled

The inspectors .... because of its poor lighting.

Part 5

For questions **40–44**, read the following texts on technological change. For questions **40–43**, answer with a word or short phrase. You do not need to write complete sentences. For question **44**, write a summary according to the instructions given.

Write your answers to questions **40–44 on the separate answer sheet**.

History is full of predictions that new machines will cause mass unemployment. In Britain in the early 19th century, a group called the Luddites smashed the new machinery that they perceived as threatening their livelihood. Similarly, in the 1930s, factory automation was blamed for high unemployment. And now doom-mongers are again predicting a jobless future as robots and computers take over. Even those lucky enough to hang on to a job will, they say, face insecurity and low wages.

If history is any guide, however, they are wrong. Over the past two centuries of huge technological advances, employment and real incomes in rich industrial countries have risen almost continuously and living standards have risen because of technological change, not in spite of it. Some of the world's most technologically advanced societies also have some of the lowest jobless rates. But modern-day Luddites remain undaunted, predicting that by the middle of the 21st century, hundreds of millions of workers will be left permanently idle.

It is true that millions of jobs will be destroyed by technology, just as they have been over the past two hundred years. But in the past, those job losses have always been offset by job gains, so total employment has continued to grow along with the population. As blacksmiths and coachmen disappeared, car mechanics and salesmen took their place. Technology changed the types of jobs on offer, but the volume continued to grow. We can expect the same pattern to be repeated in the future.   **line 19**

40 Which phrase in the first paragraph tells us the writer's view of the 'modern-day Luddites' he talks about in paragraph 2?

....

41 In your own words, explain what the writer is referring to in the phrase 'the same pattern' in line 19.

....

My friend Bill had a reel-to-reel video tape-recorder in the days before anyone imagined that VCRs would become a mainstream consumer appliance. He lusted after a personal computer in 1978, before most people even knew they existed. Now, he runs a Web-based news service and spends his days learning up-to-the-minute 'whizzeries'. Given this, you'd expect Bill to be   **line 4** the type of person who's always telling you how your latest piece of equipment has already been superseded, or that your whole way of life is going to be totally changed by the next round of innovations. But you'd be wrong. On the wall of his office, Bill has a large paper calendar, which he uses to track all his appointments. It's convenient, he says, and he can see at a glance what he's supposed to be doing on any given day. He writes on it in pencil so that it's easy to change.

Bill is, I am convinced, typical. Despite the way people talk about technological change, despite all the outlandish predictions about how it will completely change our way of life, certain things have a habit of staying much the same. In truth, new technologies rarely replace older ones completely: movies and radio weren't killed off by television, and pens and pencils are still valuable despite word processors. I bet just about everyone has somewhere a piece of obsolete technology, like Bill's calendar, kept either because it is comforting or because it does a job so extremely well that there's nothing to be gained by changing it.

42   Which word elsewhere in the first paragraph repeats the idea of 'whizzeries' in line 4?

....

43   In your own words, explain why we may be surprised to learn about Bill's calendar.

....

44   In a paragraph of between **50** and **70** words, summarise **in your own words as far as possible** the ways in which, according to the two texts, people's predictions about technological change can be wrong. Write your summary **on the separate answer sheet**.

PAPER 4   LISTENING (40 minutes approximately)

Part 1

You will hear four different extracts. For questions **1–8**, choose the answer (**A**, **B** or **C**) which fits best according to what you hear. There are two questions for each extract.

Extract 1

You hear part of a radio programme on classical music.

1 What was Carl Ruggles' attitude towards other composers?

   A   jealous
   B   resentful
   C   dismissive

2 What is the speaker doing when he speaks?

   A   summarising a musical trend
   B   providing a link for broadcast items
   C   reviewing a new recording

Extract 2

You hear part of a radio review of a French novel which has recently been translated into English.

3 The reviewer describes the babysitter in the novel as

   A   unreasonable.
   B   irresponsible.
   C   inexperienced.

4 The reviewer finds the translation of the novel unsatisfactory because

   A   it is difficult to relate to the characters.
   B   the concerns of the characters are uninteresting.
   C   the friendship between the characters is implausible.

Extract 3

You hear part of a radio programme in which a sociologist talks about bags.

5 The speaker thinks that bags are significant because

   A they are an essential accessory.
   B they protect the sensitive parts of our bodies.
   C they represent a link between different areas of our bodies.

6 The speaker's purpose in discussing the expression 'to give someone the sack' is

   A to show that bags can signify quite contradictory concepts.
   B to exemplify how language can be misused.
   C to demonstrate that the symbolism of bags crosses cultures.

Extract 4

You hear two friends talking about modern films.

7 What view of the film industry do both speakers share?

   A Studios spend too much on films.
   B Film plots are predictable.
   C Cinema audiences are more discerning.

7

8 According to the speakers, why are the facts in true stories changed for films?

   A The film makers could be sued.
   B The facts may not lend themselves to being filmed.
   C The facts could be difficult to establish.

Part 2

You will hear a scientist talking about his first visit to the Antarctic. For questions **9–17**, complete the sentences with a word or short phrase.

Richard had to undergo a survival course known as

	9

to get used to Antarctic conditions.

After his survival course, Richard was to live in a

	10

on sea ice.

There was evidence of activity from a

	11

near where the course was held.

From the area where the course took place a

	12

stretches to the South Pole.

The failure of Richard's team to construct a

	13

meant that their shelter was incomplete.

At base camp there are

	14

as well as possibilities for shopping and entertainment.

People at base camp are said to be willing to pay as much as a

	15

for a portion of salad greens.

In the hut used by the explorers Shackleton and Scott, you can see some

	16

which belonged to them.

Richard's team was named the

	17

by their course leader.

Part 3

You will hear part of a radio interview with a social worker. For questions **18–22**, choose the answer (**A**, **B**, **C** or **D**) which fits best according to what you hear.

18   What motivated Tim Jarman to change his career path?

    A   He was keen to give expert advice to his colleagues.
    B   He felt he should experience difficult conditions at first hand.
    C   He was willing to accept money from a charity.
    D   He thought it would help his academic career in the long run.

19   According to Tim, setting up the Northdown Project involved

    A   responding to suggestions from the community.
    B   organising educational activities for children.
    C   liaising closely with the local authorities.
    D   establishing relationships with existing youth clubs.

20   What did Tim feel was a crucial factor in the success of the project?

    A   A variety of sports facilities was provided.
    B   Adults were available to help with supervision.
    C   The accommodation was ideal for the project.
    D   Teenagers were allowed their own freedom.

21   In Tim's view, what influence did the Northdown Project have on most of the young people who participated in it?

    A   It encouraged them to take up worthwhile jobs.
    B   It showed them the importance of voluntary work.
    C   It helped them to lead law-abiding lives.
    D   It offered them the opportunity to meet the right partner.

22   According to Tim, there are unlikely to be more projects like the Northdown one in the near future because

    A   the need for such projects is declining.
    B   community projects are difficult to set up and fund.
    C   the current trend is for short-term projects.
    D   community groups are not interested in cooperating.

Part 4

You will hear part of a conversation in which two neighbours, Mary and Frank, are discussing current developments in museums. For questions **23–28**, decide whether the opinions are expressed by only one of the speakers, or whether the speakers agree.

Write   **M**   for Mary,
           F   for Frank,
or   **B**   for Both, where they agree.

---

23   The learning process, in general, can be enjoyable. | 23 |

24   It's a good idea to prepare children for a museum visit. | 24 |

25   Entry to museums should be free so that everybody can take advantage of them. | 25 |

26   Public libraries perform a similar function to museums. | 26 |

27   Lending out exhibits is beneficial to the wider public. | 27 |

28   The architecture of a museum affects how I view the collection. | 28 |

PAPER 5   SPEAKING
(19 minutes for pairs of candidates, 28 minutes for groups of three)

This test is also suitable for groups of three students; this only occurs at the last test of a session where a centre has an uneven number of candidates.

There are two examiners. One (the Interlocutor) conducts the test, providing you with the necessary materials and explaining what you have to do. The other examiner (the Assessor) will be introduced to you, but then takes no further part in the interaction.

Part 1 (3 minutes for pairs of candidates, 4 minutes for groups of three)

The Interlocutor first asks you and your partner(s) a few questions which focus on information about yourselves and personal opinions.

Part 2 (4 minutes for pairs of candidates, 6 minutes for groups of three)

In this part of the test you and your partner(s) are asked to talk together. The Interlocutor places a single picture or a set of pictures on the table in front of you. This stimulus provides the basis for a discussion. The Interlocutor first asks an introductory question which focuses on one or two of the pictures. After about a minute (or two for groups of three), the Interlocutor gives you both/all a decision-making task based on the same set of pictures.

The picture for Part 2 is on pages C8–C9 of the colour section.

Part 3 (12 minutes for pairs of candidates, 18 minutes for groups of three)

You are each given the opportunity to talk for two minutes, to comment after your partner has spoken and to take part in a more general discussion.

The Interlocutor gives you a card with a question written on it and asks you to talk about it for two minutes. After you have spoken, your partner is first asked to comment and then the Interlocutor asks you both another question related to the topic on the card. This procedure is repeated, so that your partner receives a card and speaks for two minutes, you are given an opportunity to comment and a follow-up question is asked. For a group of three, there is a third card and the procedure is repeated once more.

Finally, the Interlocutor asks some further questions, which leads to a discussion on a general theme related to the subjects already covered in Part 3.

The cards for Part 3 are on pages C10–C12 of the colour section.

Test 1 Key

Paper 1   Reading (1 hour 30 minutes)

Part 1   (one mark for each correct answer)
1 B   2 A   3 D   4 A   5 C   6 B   7 B   8 A   9 D
10 C   11 D   12 A   13 A   14 C   15 B   16 A
17 D   18 A

Part 2   (two marks for each correct answer)
19 B   20 C   21 C   22 D   23 C   24 D   25 C   26 B

Part 3   (two marks for each correct answer)
27 G   28 B   29 F   30 E   31 D   32 C   33 A

Part 4   (two marks for each correct answer)
34 B   35 A   36 D   37 C   38 B   39 A   40 C

Paper 2   Writing (2 hours)

Task-specific mark schemes

Question 1: Escape to the country
Content
Major points:
Discussion of   – problems of city life
                  – advantages of country life
                  – problems of country life

Further points:
Any points relevant to the area of discussion.

Range
Language for expressing and supporting opinions.

Appropriacy of register and format
Register appropriate to an article for a magazine. Article may make use of headings.

Organisation and cohesion
Clear development of arguments and ideas. Adequate use of linking and paragraphing.

Target reader
Would understand the writer's viewpoint.

Question 2: *Launching a new soft drink*

Content
Description and discussion of the different methods for advertising the soft drink, with reference to the ideas provided, and explanation as to why the writer's ideas are particularly effective.

Range
Language for describing, analysing, explaining and making recommendations.

Appropriacy of register and format
Register and format appropriate for that of a proposal – could make use of relevant section headings. Register can be formal or neutral in tone, but must be consistent.

Organisation and cohesion
Presentation of ideas and information should be well-structured. Adequate use of linking and paragraphing.

Target reader
The company would have a clear idea of what is being recommended.

Question 3: *International Festival of Drama Review*

Content
Review of the drama festival and comment on what they learned from the experience.

Range
Language of description, analysis and evaluation.

Appropriacy of register and format
Register and format should be appropriate for a review in a school/college magazine. Register can be formal/informal, but must be consistent.

Organisation and cohesion
Clear development of points. Adequate use of paragraphing and linking.

Target reader
Would be informed about the drama festival and what the writer learned from the experience.

Question 4: *College handbook for new students*

Content
Letter should give information about the college and the social organisations, and make new students feel welcome.

Range
Language for giving information.

Appropriacy of register and format
Informal/neutral, but must be consistent.
Should be encouraging and lively in tone, friendly and welcoming.

Organisation and cohesion
Well-organised, possibly with sub-headings.

Target reader
Would be well-informed about what is available at the college.

Question 5(a): The Accidental Tourist

Content
Clear reference to the book chosen.
Brief summary of the book leading to an analysis of the funny and sad elements in the story.

Range
Language of description, narration and evaluation.

Appropriacy of register and format
Review with register and format appropriate to a student magazine. Register must be consistent throughout.

Organisation and cohesion
Clear development from introduction to development of the main focus, leading to a clear conclusion.

Target reader
Would be informed about the book and appreciate both the funny and sad elements of the story.

Question 5(b): The Day of the Triffids

Content
Clear reference to the book chosen.
Description of the triffids and what they do, and discussion of their impact on society.

Range
Language of description, narration, analysis and evaluation.

Appropriacy of register and format
Neutral composition.

Organisation and cohesion
Clear presentation and development of ideas. Appropriate paragraphing and linking. Clear conclusion.

Target reader
Would be informed about the triffids and understand their role in the book.

Question 5(c): Our Man in Havana

Content
Close reference to the book chosen.
Clear focus on whether or not Wormold achieves the status of a hero.

Range
Language of description, narration and evaluation.

Appropriacy of register and format
Formal register, and format consistent and appropriate for a letter to a literary magazine.

Organisation and cohesion
Clear presentation and development of ideas, with appropriate linking and paragraphing. Clear conclusion.

Target reader
Would have a clear idea of the writer's viewpoint with regard to whether or not Wormold achieves the status of a hero.

Paper 3   Use of English (1 hour 30 minutes)

Part 1   (one mark for each correct answer)

1 back   2 part   3 it   4 there   5 against / to   6 little
7 brought   8 until / till   9 that   10 to   11 went
12 would / could / might   13 means   14 hardly / scarcely
15 so / as / that

Part 2   (one mark for each correct answer)

16 invariably   17 pressure   18 excessive   19 essential
20 retailers   21 centrally   22 illogical   23 unavoidable
24 criticism(s)   25 efficiency

Part 3   (two marks for each correct answer)

26 matter   27 flat   28 fell   29 beat   30 led   31 press

Part 4   (one mark for each correct section)

32 no (previous) time (before) (1) + has the present government (ever) (1)
33 is / seems to be (rather / somewhat) lacking (in) (1) + clarity / cohesion (1)
34 not to (1) + take sides (1)
35 to meet (1) + anyone / anybody / someone / somebody (who is) more generous than OR + a more generous person than (1)
36 reveal / manifest / show / display / demonstrate / have the slightest hesitation in OR hesitate in the slightest (1)
   + when it came to OR before / about (1)
37 (had) never crossed (1) + my mind (1)
38 (the reason) why Liz (should have) left / departed (1) + (so) suddenly (1)
39 had (finally) run (1) + out of (1)

Part 5   (questions 40–43 two marks for each correct answer)

40 analogy of market place particularly appropriate in a business text

115

41 they are arrived at by chance or are a reflection of the personality of the person in charge of the company

42 their personal goals coincide with company goals so they can work on both at the same time

43 workers are not permitted to develop and implement their own ideas for improvement, thus restricting company development
no group vision

44 (one mark for each content point, up to ten marks for summary skills)
The paragraph should include the following points:
   i   both need to be in good shape / have level of fitness
   ii require mental determination to succeed
  iii perform better as a team
  iv need to raise the level of objectives when they are approached so that progress continues to be made / reassess their goals continually

Paper 4   Listening (40 minutes approximately)

Part 1   (one mark for each correct answer)
1 A   **2** B   **3** B   **4** B   **5** C   **6** A   **7** A   **8** B

Part 2   (one mark for each correct answer)
9 transporting goods   **10** (welcome) shelter   **11** copper
12 ice(-)dance / ice(-)dancing   **13** air(-)conditioning / air conditioners
14 spray   **15** logo(s)   **16** 20 / twenty hours   **17** fog

Part 3   (one mark for each correct answer)
18 B   **19** C   **20** A   **21** D   **22** C

Part 4   (one mark for each correct answer)
23 B   **24** A   **25** A   **26** C   **27** B   **28** C

Transcript   *Certificate of Proficiency in English Listening Test. Test 1.*

I'm going to give you the instructions for this test.

I'll introduce each part of the test and give you time to look at the questions.

At the start of each piece you'll hear this sound:

tone

You'll hear each piece twice.

Remember, while you're listening, write your answers on the question paper.

You'll have five minutes at the end of the test to copy your answers onto the separate answer sheet.

There will now be a pause. You must ask any questions now, because you must not speak during the test.

[pause]

PART 1   *Now open your question paper and look at Part One.*

[pause]

You'll hear four different extracts. For questions 1 to 8, choose the answer (A, B or C) which fits best according to what you hear. There are two questions for each extract.

Extract 1   [pause]

tone

Presenter: Do you *have* to do all these interviews to publicise the film, Tom? Is it in your contract?

Actor: No, but I feel it's part of my responsibility to advertise it. Having done a few low-budget films that come out for a week and then disappear, it's really disappointing. So you go on and do the local radio so that people come and see it, especially if it's something that you're proud of. I think you often find that if an actor isn't prepared to do an interview, it's more often than not because they're not happy with themselves or the product.

Presenter: Sometimes with the big stars there's this long list of things we're not allowed to ask them about!

Actor: That's not fair, is it? If they say they're going to do the interview, then they should. If you were to ask me an incredibly awkward question, I could just say, 'Well, I don't want to talk about that'. But as I say, I'm here to plug the film! I mean, I'm not here to make myself a big celebrity or anything. That's what . . .

[pause]

tone

[The recording is repeated.]

[pause]

Extract 2   [pause]

tone

How would you describe your personality? Anxious? Outgoing? The list could be quite long. In fact, psychologists have found approaching 18,000 words to describe personality. If so much of our language is given over to this activity, then the description of personality must be an important part of everyday life. But perhaps we are influenced in the way we judge another's character by our general liking or disliking for them. A beloved uncle is eccentric, whereas a more unpopular one is mad. So clearly there are advantages to the scientific study of personality.

As one interesting example of what's been discovered, take extroversion and introversion. Extroversion means being very outward-looking, sociable, noisy, and introversion is the opposite. Originally, it was thought that people fell into one or other of these two groups. But now all studies of personality show that they are not separate categories, but represent the two extremes of a continuum, and that in fact most people are somewhere in the middle.

[pause]

tone

[The recording is repeated.]

[pause]

Extract 3   [pause]

tone

When I think of my childhood home now, it seems that its beauty is protected by its remoteness and that very remoteness made me want not so much to leave, but escape. The corner of Scotland I come from is a peninsula cut off from the rest of Scotland by the sea and the stark emptiness of the moors.

Last summer I went home and tried insanely to buy a house. I'd been nurturing this idea for some time. The moment I set eyes on the house, I knew it was for me, as though the hand of destiny had guided me down the track.

What was I thinking? – I had no livelihood there. I was a foreign correspondent whose only specialism was international affairs. My 'home' and everything I knew best was in London. The house was built of granite and seemed to grow organically from the rock, as though it was part of the natural topography. It was timeless, unchanging, predictable and certain, just what I was seeking. I made an offer on it, which wasn't accepted. I was saved from my own sentimental folly.

[pause]

tone

[The recording is repeated.]

[pause]

Extract 4   [pause]

tone

Interviewer: So, why did you decide to write this book on the USA **now**?
Author: Well a few years ago, when I was there, I was asked to write a book about it; and I must have spent at least four or five minutes contemplating this exercise. The States is more like a world than a country; you could as well write a book about people, or about life. There's so much material – it's all embracing. Then, years later, as I was emptying out my desk drawers to gather together a selection of past pieces I'd written, I found that I'd already written a book about the US, but it was unpremeditated, accidental, and in instalments. Of the hundreds of thousands of words I seem to have written for newspapers and magazines in the last fifteen years, about half of them seem to be about the US. But I hope these disparate pieces add up to something. I know you can approach the subject only if you come at it from at least a dozen different directions.

[pause]

tone

[The recording is repeated.]

That's the end of Part One.

Now turn to Part Two.

PART 2

[pause]

You will hear part of a radio programme about ice-skating rinks. For questions 9 to 17, complete the sentences with a word or short phrase.

You now have forty-five seconds in which to look at Part Two.

[pause]

tone

If you've ever been to watch any of Britain's professional ice-hockey teams, you've no doubt thrilled at the speed and agility of great athletes skating on indoor ice. But you've probably taken for granted the surface that makes it all possible. Nevertheless, the temperature and other characteristics of the surface can make the difference between a championship-winning performance and an embarrassing spill. Indoor ice rinks are used for all sorts of sports and recreational activities, in all of which the quality of the ice makes a big difference.

Ice-skating began as a means of transporting goods on the frozen rivers and canals throughout northern Europe long before anyone ever saw it as the recreational activity which it later became. Considering that skating for pleasure was done outdoors in the freezing winter weather, it's fair to say that indoor ice rinks were created because in those conditions they provided welcome shelter for those who enjoyed skating. It was only when ice became available year-round that sports such as hockey and skating had a chance to flourish.

In 1876 the first indoor rink opened in London, although the idea was not replicated up and down the country as had been predicted, as the process entailed making the ice by pumping a mixture of glycerine and water through copper pipes, a material which was expensive at that time. The first Olympic figure-skating competition was held on a refrigerated indoor rink as part of the Summer Games in London in 1908, though it was not until 1976 that ice-dancing, that is, interpreting music on skates, became a Winter Olympics sport. In the early twentieth century, electric refrigeration and indoor rinks made ice-skating popular everywhere.

The technology that makes indoor rinks possible is also found in refrigerators and air conditioning in our homes. In an indoor ice rink, the refrigerant doesn't cool the ice directly, as home systems do. Instead, it cools salt water that is pumped through an intricate system of pipes underneath the ice.

Laying down a good skating surface isn't as simple as making a tray of ice cubes. Freezing a rink correctly takes no less than a dozen stages, with some stages laying ice that is wafer thin. And what's best for one sport may be completely unacceptable for another! It takes up to seventy thousand litres of water to make a rink. The first two layers of ice, which are less than one millimetre thick, are applied via a spray to create a fine mist of water. The first layer freezes almost immediately after it's sprayed on, and then the second is applied. The second frozen layer is painted white, allowing for a strong contrast, for example, in hockey, between the black disc known as the puck and the ice. The third layer acts as a sealer for the paint. This layer then requires painting to create decorative backgrounds and, in the case of hockey, provide clear markings and display sponsors' logos. Once all the markings have dried, the final layer is gradually applied. This uses forty thousand litres of water which must be put on slowly with a hose at a rate of two to three thousand litres per hour. That means at least 15, at most 20 hours for this final layer. The less water is put on the floor at one time, the better the ice will be.

Brand new ice is called green ice because it hasn't been broken in yet. When creating a new rink, indoor conditions are very important, with the skating surface kept at −4.5 to −3° Celsius, the building temperature at about 17° Celsius, and the indoor humidity at about 30%. But if it's warm outdoors, the temperature has to be re-adjusted accordingly. Even one degree can make a big difference in the quality of the ice. In addition, a fog over the ice can be created by high humidity indoors which, of course, would hold a hockey game up.

So, on a hot summer's day when you…

[pause]

Now you'll hear Part Two again.

tone

[The recording is repeated.]

[pause]

That's the end of Part Two.

Now turn to Part Three.

[pause]

PART 3   *You will hear the beginning of a radio interview with Stephen Perrins, a composer of musicals. For questions 18 to 22, choose the answer (A, B, C or D) which fits best according to what you hear.*

You now have one minute in which to look at Part Three.

[pause]

tone

Interviewer: My guest today started out in the world of serious music and showed great promise as an avant garde composer, but he made the surprising leap into the world of the musical theatre. Welcome, Stephen Perrins.

Stephen Perrins: Thank you.

Interviewer: Stephen, what made you change from serious music to musicals?

Stephen Perrins: Well, my parents were both professors of music, so I dutifully went to music college, studied composition, and wrote rather inaccessible music. But I suppose really my heart's always been in the theatre, and I soon found myself writing songs in secret, drawing my inspiration from musicals.

Interviewer: Did you try to get them published?

Stephen Perrins:	No, for a long time I kept them to myself, even though I thought they were commercial. I suppose I had something of an inferiority complex about them, because they were a bit slushy, and I was sure my family and college would think they were below me.
Interviewer:	So what happened?
Stephen Perrins:	Well, we had a very light-hearted end-of-year show at college, and I decided, more or less on impulse, to sing one of my songs, because it happened to fit rather neatly into a sketch that Jenny Fisher and I wrote, which was a spoof opera. And it kind of stole the show. A year later a schoolteacher friend, who'd been in the cast, got in touch with me – he wanted a short musical for a concert at his school. In fact, just as an experiment, Jenny and I had already worked up the opera sketch into something we renamed *Goldringer*, without any real idea of what to do with it next, so it just needed a bit of tinkering.
Interviewer:	That was lucky.
Stephen Perrins:	The real break was that the music critic of a national paper had a child at the school, and the following Sunday we read this rave review saying that Jenny and I were the future of the musical, and of course we were on cloud nine, and we immediately had music publishers lining up.
Interviewer:	How did your family react?
Stephen Perrins:	Oh, they were aghast at first, but they came round, and they've been right behind us ever since.
Interviewer:	You've always said you won't do the lyrics of your songs. I presume you've tried.
Stephen Perrins:	I did with my early songs. In fact I could knock them off with a rather suspect facility. But I realised that if I wrote both the words and the music I'd be working in a kind of vacuum, and what I enjoy most is the collaboration and sparking off each other's ideas.
Interviewer:	There was a story in the papers recently that you wanted to direct your musicals, too. Has anything come of that?
Stephen Perrins:	No, that just wasn't true. I never claim to be a director, I always think when you've actually appointed the director for a show, you shouldn't undermine them. For example, in one of my shows, which Helen Downes directed, I wasn't that happy with the design, but she was passionate to have it, and it was right not to interfere.
Interviewer:	Now in the last few years you've had great international success, but for some of the more upmarket newspapers, it seems, you simply can't put a foot right.
Stephen Perrins:	No, and I don't really know quite why. Maybe I'm being big-headed, but I don't think it's because of the music. I think it's more that I'm not really that bothered about my image, so I don't do masses of PR. Which means I leave myself open to that carping sort of criticism.
Interviewer:	It seems to me it's a kind of distaste for the popularity of your music.
Stephen Perrins:	It's like the time when serious art critics looked down on the late 19th-century artists, and their paintings were considered worthless. The fact is that if you went into an art gallery, guess where the public were.
Interviewer:	Just as the public are always to be found at your musicals. Stephen Perrins, thank you.
Stephen Perrins:	Thank you.

[pause]

Now you'll hear Part Three again.

tone

[The recording is repeated.]

[pause]

That's the end of Part Three.

Now turn to Part Four.

PART 4   [pause]

You will hear part of a radio arts programme, in which two people, Arthur and Carla, are discussing a book called Windworld. For questions 23 to 28, decide whether the opinions are expressed by only one of the speakers, or whether the speakers agree. Write A for Arthur, C for Carla, or B for both, where they agree.

You now have thirty seconds in which to look at Part Four.

[pause]

tone

Presenter: Today on *A Good Read* we are talking about George Swallow's novel *Windworld*, published last year and it has just won the Bateman Prize. We have with us Arthur Lachman, writer, and Carla Fletcher, who lectures in Engineering at King's College. Arthur, let's start with you...

Arthur: Well, I read the novel when it first came out and I was very happy to be asked to re-read it for this programme and I remembered the powerful characterisation – the certainty of touch – particularly of the older protagonist, Joe Bean, and his sisters, in the throes of change from one era to another.

Carla: Rather miserable characters but assured portraits.

Arthur: Mmmm... What I valued as well was the atmosphere Swallow creates, the sense that everything he created felt right within the time and place. Did you find that?

Carla: Very interesting question. As a scientist, I always come to books with a critical eye for technical details. As I say, Joe Bean and his family as *people* rang incredibly true for me. I found myself doubting whether certain incidents, ummm... certain assumptions squared with the period in which the book is set.

Arthur: I have to say that I found the sheer amount of technical detail about inventions, which Swallow included as a labour of love, I have no doubt, gave the lay person a hard time, making it difficult to follow the plot.

Carla: Umm. I actually found myself comparing all these descriptions of the windmills and pumps with... with his earlier works *Learner Games* and *Thorn*... which both dealt with the same period but neither of which included this kind of complexity. Much more populist... deliberately more accessible to a wide readership.

Arthur: There is much to *link* the writing of all three books: you can recognise Swallow's individual voice in all of them – he's speaking to one specific audience in my view.

Presenter: Do you feel *Windworld* is a great novel?

Arthur: Oh very much so. The current of the author's own life in the East of England pulses through the whole work so compellingly. So, yes, I would say that it lifts this book... ummm... into the category of great writing.

Carla: I wouldn't be quite that positive, though I do agree that the character of Joe Bean draws its strength from the writer's close acquaintance with Joe's environment: to my mind he's almost certainly Swallow putting himself in another age – positioning himself, with his upbringing and his character and his beliefs, in the 18th century.

Arthur: I was intrigued by some of these set episodes, like the incident with the birds. It was genuinely fascinating, I thought. I understand the film rights have been bought. Do you think it'll work as well as the book does?

Carla: No question – if they keep away from too much social realism and misery. If they don't make Joe's story the central one, it'll die a death.

Arthur: Well – just about all the stories are likely to come through well, in my opinion. We'll have to see how it turns out!

[pause]

Now you'll hear Part Four again.

tone

[The recording is repeated.]

[pause]

That's the end of Part Four.

There will now be a pause of five minutes for you to copy your answers onto the separate answer sheet. Be sure to follow the numbering of all the questions. I'll remind you when there is one minute left, so that you're sure to finish in time.

[pause]

You have one more minute left.

[pause]

That's the end of the test. Please stop now. Your supervisor will now collect all the question papers and answer sheets.

Test 2 Key

Paper 1   Reading (1 hour 30 minutes)

Part 1   (one mark for each correct answer)

1 B   2 C   3 A   4 D   5 A   6 B   7 B   8 D   9 A
10 B   11 C   12 A   13 B   14 A   15 C   16 A
17 C   18 A

Part 2   (two marks for each correct answer)

19 A   20 D   21 C   22 D   23 A   24 D   25 B   26 A

Part 3   (two marks for each correct answer)

27 B   28 H   29 G   30 E   31 A   32 F   33 C

Part 4   (two marks for each correct answer)

34 D   35 B   36 A   37 C   38 A   39 D   40 C

Paper 2   Writing (2 hours)

Task-specific mark schemes

Question 1: Growing old

Content
Major points:
Discussion of: – whether or not old people have something useful to offer society
– whether or not other people have to look after old people
– the advantages and disadvantages that belong to old age

Further points:
Relevant examples to support either or both of the views expressed.

Range
Language for expressing and supporting opinions, and for expressing agreement and disagreement.

Appropriacy of register and format
Formal/semi-formal letter format. Register appropriate to the writer's role as reader of a magazine writing in to express opinions.

Organisation and cohesion
Clear organisation of points. Adequate use of paragraphing and linking.

Target reader
Would understand the writer's viewpoint.

Question 2: Differences between rich and poor

Content

There may be some brief introduction to the causes of poverty, but the main content should be suggestions on ways of helping to reduce the differences between rich and poor, plus comments on why these ideas might work.

Range

Language for describing, analysing, evaluating and making recommendations.

Appropriacy of register and format

Register and format appropriate for that of a proposal – could make use of relevant section headings. Register can be formal or neutral in tone, but must be consistent.

Organisation and cohesion

Presentation of ideas and information should be well-structured. Adequate use of linking and paragraphing.

Target reader

The reader would have a clear idea of what suggestions are being made.

Question 3: New leisure centre, library or playground?

Content

Description and analysis of what local residents think about the three proposals, including recommendations based on the opinions that local residents have expressed.

Range

Language of description, analysis and recommendation.

Appropriacy of register and format

Register and format appropriate for a report for the local council – could make use of section headings. Register must be consistent.

Organisation and cohesion

Clear organisation of content with adequate use of linking and paragraphing.

Target reader

The local council would have a clear idea of what the local residents think the money should be spent on.

Question 4: 'A Country of Contrasts'

Content

Description of the different types of places that can be found.
Opinions about these different places.
Opinion of how these contrasts make the country an interesting place to visit.

Range

Language of description, comparison and opinion.

Appropriacy of register and format
Appropriate to an article in a travel magazine.

Organisation and cohesion
Magazine-style article possibly with headings to introduce different places.

Target reader
Would want to visit the country because of the contrasts and have a clear idea of what the contrasts were.

Question 5(a): The Accidental Tourist

Content
Clear reference to the book chosen.
Evaluation of the statement and whether or not it is true.

Range
Language of description, narration and evaluation.

Appropriacy of register and format
Neutral essay.

Organisation and cohesion
Clear presentation and development of ideas. Appropriate paragraphing and linking. Clear conclusion.

Target reader
Would understand the viewpoint of the writer with regard to Macon.

Question 5(b): The Day of the Triffids

Content
Clear reference to the book chosen.
Description of events that changed the world, and an evaluation of whether or not the book gives an optimistic view of human nature.

Range
Language of description, narration and evaluation.

Appropriacy of register and format
Review with register and format appropriate for a literary magazine. Register must be consistent throughout.

Organisation and cohesion
Clear development from introduction to development of the main focus, leading to a clear conclusion.

Target reader
Would have a clear understanding of the writer's viewpoint.

Question 5(c): Our Man in Havana

Content

Close reference to the book chosen. Evaluation of whether the statement is true or not. Reference to what is amusing and entertaining in the book, and whether or not it has a serious moral purpose. Both parts of the question need to be addressed.

Range

Language of description, narration and evaluation.

Appropriacy of register and format

Clear presentation and development of ideas. Appropriate paragraphing and linking. The two parts of the question can be dealt with separately or together. Clear conclusion.

Organisation and cohesion

Neutral essay.

Target reader

Would understand the viewpoint of the writer.

Paper 3   Use of English (1 hour 30 minutes)

Part 1   (one mark for each correct answer)

1 one / that   2 only NOT just   3 how   4 other   5 should
6 from   7 such   8 with   9 not   10 regard / respect / reference
NOT answers   11 none / nothing   12 far   13 however
14 may / might / would   15 though / as

Part 2   (one mark for each correct answer)

16 regularity   17 justice   18 mathematicians   19 repeatedly
20 unravel   21 breakthroughs   22 meteorology   23 spectacular
24 awesome   25 disclose

Part 3   (two marks for each correct answer)

26 short   27 rough   28 covered   29 touched   30 track
31 question

Part 4   (one mark for each correct section)

32 as I enjoy / like reading, (1) + there are times when / that OR at times (1)
33 had been published / was published (1) + did the president make (1)
34 been for your support (1) + I'd still be (1)
35 expressed / voiced / made clear (1) + (their) disapproval of / about (1)
36 as no surprise to me (1) + to hear about / of (1)
37 ought to / should / had / 'd better say / mention (1) + anything / a word about (1)
38 (completely / totally) at a (total / complete) loss (1) + to explain / understand / know / account for (the reason) as to / over (the reason) (1)
39 Minister's resignation (1) + resulted from (1)

Part 5   (questions 40–43 two marks for each correct answer)

40 his wife gets angry and his children are contemptuous / mocking / insult him
41 they cannot be stopped
42 they are (self-sufficient) loners
43 more facilities would avoid overcrowding and therefore increase enjoyment
44 (one mark for each content point, up to ten marks for summary skills)
    The paragraph should include the following points:
   i the need to be alone / get away from others
   ii personal challenge
   iii the pleasure of being in the fresh air
   iv the need for stimulation / uplift / curiosity brought by new scenes and activities

Paper 4   Listening (40 minutes approximately)

Part 1   (one mark for each correct answer)

1 B   2 A   3 C   4 A   5 C   6 B   7 C   8 A

Part 2   (one mark for each correct answer)

9 zoology   10 (human) eye(s)   11 feathers
12 bee   13 rescuers / rescue(-)teams   14 (a) low speed / low speeds
15 energy source / battery   16 take(-)off / taking off   17 (the) noise

Part 3   (one mark for each correct answer)

18 B   19 A   20 B   21 C   22 A

Part 4   (one mark for each correct answer)

23 G   24 M   25 B   26 B   27 G   28 M

Transcript   *Certificate of Proficiency in English Listening Test. Test 2.*

I'm going to give you the instructions for this test.

I'll introduce each part of the test and give you time to look at the questions.

At the start of each piece you'll hear this sound:

tone

You'll hear each piece twice.

Remember, while you're listening, write your answers on the question paper.

You'll have five minutes at the end of the test to copy your answers onto the separate answer sheet.

There will now be a pause. You must ask any questions now, because you must not speak during the test.

[pause]

Now open your question paper and look at Part One.

[pause]

PART 1 *You'll hear four different extracts. For questions 1 to 8, choose the answer (A, B or C) which fits best according to what you hear. There are two questions for each extract.*

Extract 1 [pause]

tone

Interviewer: So, finally Nigel, you achieved your ambition and made the break into films. It seems to me you got a lot of stick about it, I mean, on the one hand from jealous film makers, which is understandable, but also, more interestingly, from the literary community in Ireland, who seemed to be upset that you were doing something quite so vulgar. Although presumably it's good for the way Ireland is perceived abroad.

Nigel: That's perfectly true. But you know, at the time, novelists didn't make films. Now it's quite a common thing.

Interviewer: But isn't it that rather conservative, orthodox Irish thing that serious writers don't stray away from the high realm of literature?

Nigel: I wouldn't call it conservative and orthodox. I would say actually that the importance of writing in Irish culture is huge. It's always been the subversive force in the culture itself.

Interviewer: But conservative in the sense that you're not allowed to do anything else if that's what you're capable of doing.

Nigel: Well, it's kind of seen as a vocation in a way, I suppose.

[pause]

tone

[The recording is repeated.]

[pause]

Extract 2 [pause]

tone

Woman: Do you know, an amazing thing happened to me yesterday: two totally unconnected people looked me straight in the eye and told me they were sorry!

Man: No!

Woman: Honest! You know I have a permit to park outside my flat?

Man: Yes?

Woman: Well I was sent a new one in January, but some idiot had written the wrong year on it, and I was fined for parking illegally.

Man: Oh no!

Woman: So I went storming into the town hall, spluttering with rage. And would you believe, the woman behind the desk not only said sorry, but owned up that she recognised her writing. It really took the wind out of my sails, and I found myself clucking sympathetically and saying what an easy mistake it was to make! Then in the afternoon I had someone coming round to repair my cooker, and he turned up three hours late. I went ballistic when he arrived, but he apologised for disrupting my day, and I stopped frothing at the mouth. Then his company rang, and it turned out it wasn't even his fault, so of course I felt I'd made a real fool of myself!

[pause]

tone

[The recording is repeated.]

[pause]

Extract 3 [pause]

tone

Have you ever wondered why something makes you laugh? Human beings love to laugh so much that there are actually industries built around laughter. For us it seems so natural, but laughter is a distinctly human response. Philosopher John Morreall believes that the first human laughter may have begun as a gesture of shared relief at the passing of danger. The relaxation that results from a bout of laughter inhibits the biological fight-or-flight response, laughter may signal trust in one's companions. Studies have also found that dominant individuals – whether boss, tribal chief or family patriarch – use humour more than their subordinates. If you've often thought that people at work laugh sycophantically when the boss laughs, you're very perceptive. In such cases, Morreall says, controlling the laughter of a group becomes a way of exercising power by controlling the group dynamics. So laughter, like much human behaviour, must have evolved to influence the way people interact. And there have been numerous interesting...

[pause]

tone

[The recording is repeated.]

[pause]

Extract 4 [pause]

tone

One day in 1993 I got a call from TV producer Tim Taylor, asking me to meet him to discuss a new series popularising history. I'd never heard of Tim but he explained historian Mike Lewis was the other person fronting the programme. I'd met Mike before and couldn't think of anyone I'd rather embark on a project with. We met and, though I had some reservations about the way it would all turn out, I agreed to sign up for the pilot programme, hoping that the TV company would like this initial episode.

Now the problem with a pilot is that everyone knows best – until it's finished you can't tell who's right. We weren't confident that history alone would galvanise an audience. My experience of storytelling might prove useful in getting history across. I thought this was a great idea and got really engrossed in my solo about a fanatical medieval monk. Looking back, this does look terribly self-indulgent and reduces the programme to a snail's crawl. But we submitted it to the broadcasters who were critical of this, but they offered us a series and the rest is history – quite literally!

[pause]

tone

[The recording is repeated.]

[pause]

That's the end of Part One.

Now turn to Part Two.

[pause]

PART 2   *You will hear an engineer giving a talk on the radio about future developments in robot design. For questions 9 to 17, complete the sentences with a word or short phrase.*

You now have forty-five seconds in which to look at Part Two.

[pause]

tone

By dint of brute force and massive use of external energy we can outpace all other animals, but when it comes to sheer finesse and the use of cunning tricks of aerodynamics, the animal kingdom leaves us standing. Increasingly, engineers are looking to zoology for clues on improving performance or making robots that can cope with harsh environments. But although it takes modern science to fathom exactly how animals do things, there's nothing new about the basic principle of trying to copy nature. For instance would we have tried so hard to create flying machines if it wasn't for the example of birds? But in the early days of aeronautical engineering, scientists had inadequate observation techniques, they relied solely on the human eye. Initially, as a consequence of that, they thought that the secret of how birds flew lay in the flapping movements that they made and the pattern of feathers alone. If they'd looked at the *right* aspects of engineering and bird flight, they would have achieved powered flight and manned flight earlier.

Interestingly, flapping wings are now making a comeback. After a century in which powered flight used only fixed and rotating wings, engineers are rediscovering the benefits of how insects fly. They're trying to produce a fifteen-centimetre flying robot, derived in part from the bee. The potential uses of such a machine are limited only by the imagination. For example, it could be used where buildings have collapsed and there are possible casualties to be rescued. If a person is trapped and is still breathing, then there is an opening through which air is coming in and a robot could fly in through this opening and take a photograph

131

which would help the rescuers to assess the position and plan the operation better.

But why model the robot on insect flight at all? The answer to this is that only an insect is up to the demands of the job. If you think of working inside buildings, manoeuvring at low speeds is essential because otherwise the robot will collide with obstructions. It will need to be able to hover, because if it finds something of interest, it will have to stay still to take a clear picture of it. And finally, and this is a very important requirement, the robot must fly in a power-efficient way, because it will be fairly small so there won't be much space to put in an energy source. So the first thought of the design team was to use some conventional design like a fixed-wing forward thrust, as in the usual plane, or alternatively, rotary wings, found in a helicopter, and scale them down to fifteen centimetres. The problem is that planes require considerable speed to achieve take-off, so they can't fly very slowly and also they can't hover or manoeuvre in a very agile way. So would helicopters be more appropriate? They can certainly fly very slowly and hover and they are very manoeuvrable, but they have other problems: they generate considerable noise, so that would rule out any situations where the robots would need to remain undetected such as in undercover surveillance or data gathering projects. So, having eliminated the tried and tested designs, the question was what other proven design was there? In 300 million years flapping-wing insects have certainly proved their efficiency. They offer agility even at low speed, they can do amazing aerobatics, they can hover, and unlike helicopters their flight mechanism generates very little noise.

There's more to insect flight than just flapping wings though. The movements of those wings are remarkably complex. For engineers to create a successful flying robot they will have to draw on the accumulated knowledge of zoologists. It's going to be a hard but fascinating journey of discovery.

[pause]

Now you'll hear Part Two again.

tone

[The recording is repeated.]

[pause]

That's the end of Part Two.

Now turn to Part Three.

[pause]

PART 3

You will hear a radio interview with a music critic, Hazel Fisher, about some classical music awards. For questions 18 to 22, choose the answer (A, B, C or D) which fits best according to what you hear.

You now have one minute in which to look at Part Three.

[pause]

tone

Presenter:	Now here's our regular critic Hazel Fisher, who's been invited to vote in a new initiative, the Classical Music Awards. Hazel, giving awards for classical music is surely a healthy development, isn't it?
Hazel:	On the face of it, yes. When these awards were announced recently, it seemed like a genuinely enlightened idea. There's the prospect of a huge amount of publicity surrounding the event, so it seemed like a high-profile boost for the serious classical market.
Presenter:	And it's well-timed, too, isn't it?
Hazel:	Very well-timed, because a lot of people don't hold out much hope for classical music sales. Here at last, I thought, would be recognition for all those small record companies who continue to produce worthwhile releases, while the major companies are just concerned with a safe repertoire and endlessly reissuing their old recordings. And at the same time, it would help all those performers who produce excellent music without any of the trappings of jetset celebrity. You know, it makes me so cross that the glossiest new recordings nowadays are usually turned into an international circus of the same bankable names. It certainly wouldn't come amiss if a wider range of performers were brought into the limelight for a change.
Presenter:	So why did your enthusiasm evaporate?
Hazel:	It was when the list of nominations was announced. It was clear that the whole exercise was nothing more than a cynical marketing exercise, with two aims. One was to eat even further into the distinction between what's worthwhile and what's just opportunistic rubbish. And the second was to bolster the sales of the industry's heavyweight companies, who have invested so heavily in these crossover products, that won't stand the test of time.
Presenter:	Crossover?
Hazel:	That's when classical singers, orchestras, and so on, play non-classical music, like musicals or pop or jazz.
Presenter:	Right. Now, you also object to the way the final choices are going to be made, don't you?
Hazel:	Yes, I do. Ten nominations've been made in each category, and the winners will be chosen by an 'academy' of recording industry stalwarts. So if there's no bias there, I will eat my hat. It hasn't been made public how the voting will work, but rumour has it that it's pretty opaque, though designed to be as fair as possible. Goodness knows how long the whole thing will take, especially as there are a lot of sections, but that's their problem. They've allowed several months before the awards ceremony.
Presenter:	And what do you think about the nominations themselves?
Hazel:	I find those absolutely mind-boggling. It's still a mystery who actually compiled these shortlists, but they would have us believe that film music and other lightweight work are among the ten best 'classical' albums of the year. And the fact that they only include one or two genuine classical items in each list shows what they're really interested in. For instance, take the Male Artist of the Year category: it's beyond me how anyone can choose between, say, a singer specialising in 17th and 18th century operas and a composer of film scores. It would take a more sophisticated knowledge of the musical world than I have.
Presenter:	So what's your verdict?

Hazel: Well, it's hard to escape the conclusion that the organising group, and the record companies that constitute it, are happy to move the goalposts whenever it suits them commercially. Which brings up a wonderful irony too. Recently the record companies have been complaining bitterly because a CD of popular classics given a synthesiser makeover was included in the classical bestsellers chart. But now they seem only too happy to go along with this farrago, which does more to confuse the boundaries between what's classical and what's popular (if that's the right classification) than any amount of synthesiser doodlings.

Presenter: But do you think we should even care about it at all?

[pause]

Now you'll hear Part Three again.

tone

[The recording is repeated.]

[pause]

That's the end of Part Three.

Now turn to Part Four.

[pause]

PART 4 *You will hear two neighbours, Graham and Melinda, discussing changes that the town council are making to a public park near their homes. For questions 23 to 28, decide whether the opinions are expressed by only one of the speakers, or whether the speakers agree. Write G from Graham, M for Melinda, or B for both, where they agree.*

You now have thirty seconds in which to look at Part Four.

[pause]

tone

Graham: Have you seen what's happening in Baxton Park, Melinda? The town council's put all this fencing round so you can't get in. And they've brought in an earthmover to churn up all the grass and level the ground. It looks awful!

Melinda: Oh I know. It *is* a pity. It used to belong to some member of the aristocracy, you know, as part of her land, about a hundred years ago.

Graham: Yes, I think I heard that somewhere.

Melinda: Apparently she gave it to the people of Baxton for their 'recreational use'. That's what she said in her will.

Graham: Oh did she? But then surely they can't go ahead with developing it? She can't have wanted it dug up like this! It's against the terms of the will!

Melinda: I suppose it depends what you mean by 'recreational use', doesn't it? It could mean for sport, couldn't it? And we know they're going to put two football pitches and a cricket ground on it.

Graham: Yes, *and* what they call a hospitality building right in the middle. That's being paid for by one of the local companies, you know.

Melinda:	Oh dear! I can just see it being used to host parties every weekend, and then people'll be coming and going at all hours of the night! How are we ever going to get a decent night's sleep?
Graham:	Oh, I think the trees will probably muffle the sound quite a bit, after all they're quite dense round here. I'm more worried about the parking. This is going to attract a lot of people and the road's busy enough as it is.
Melinda:	I know, I often have difficulty finding a space. I mean it took me a quarter of an hour the other day. What really gets me is the way all this has been managed. It's so underhand! I mean, we scotched the plan when it surfaced five years ago, and now, without a word of warning to any of us locals, it's reared its ugly head again.
Graham:	We really should have been given the chance to have our say, shouldn't we? That's the least you'd expect. You know, I was just wondering...
Melinda:	What? Go on.
Graham:	Well, of course, it's just a suspicion, I haven't any proof as such, but I was just wondering if anybody on the council had been, you know, got at by the developers. I mean, it's quite a big project. There'll be some lucrative contracts in there.
Melinda:	You're getting paranoid, Graham! Been watching too many movies about big business! No, I think we just have to accept it. There's nothing any of us can do about it.
Graham:	What about calling a protest meeting? We could phone up the local paper and get their photographer round. You never know, we might just get them to think again.
Melinda:	Oh yes? And do you really think that's going to get us anywhere?
Graham:	Well OK, just a thought.
Melinda:	Maybe we should try looking on the bright side...

[pause]

Now you'll hear Part Four again.

tone

[The recording is repeated.]

[pause]

That's the end of Part Four.

There will now be a pause of five minutes for you to copy your answers onto the separate answer sheet. Be sure to follow the numbering of all the questions. I'll remind you when there is one minute left, so that you're sure to finish in time.

[pause]

You have one more minute left.

[pause]

That's the end of the test. Please stop now. Your supervisor will now collect all the question papers and answer sheets.

Test 3 Key

Paper 1   Reading (1 hour 30 minutes)

Part 1   (one mark for each correct answer)

1 A   2 B   3 B   4 A   5 C   6 D   7 A   8 B   9 A
10 C   11 B   12 D   13 D   14 C   15 B   16 A
17 C   18 D

Part 2   (two marks for each correct answer)

19 C   20 A   21 B   22 A   23 B   24 D   25 B   26 D

Part 3   (two marks for each correct answer)

27 G   28 E   29 B   30 H   31 D   32 A   33 C

Part 4   (two marks for each correct answer)

34 A   35 C   36 C   37 D   38 B   39 C   40 B

Paper 2   Writing (2 hours)

Task-specific mark schemes

Question 1: Employment in the future

Content
Major points:
Discussion of: – whether or not unemployment will continue to rise as a result of the increasing use of machines/computers and the need for profits
     – whether or not new developments will create new job opportunities
     – the writer's own viewpoint on the matter

Range
Language for expressing and supporting opinions, and for reaching conclusions.

Appropriacy of register and format
Formal essay-type register.
Register appropriate to the writer's role as a student.

Organisation and cohesion
Clear organisation of points. Adequate use of linking and paragraphing
Logical development of argument and clear conclusion(s).

Target reader
The tutor would understand the writer's viewpoint.

Question 2: 'Healthy Lifestyles for the Young' magazine

Content
Should discuss possible coverage of health and lifestyle issues, and ideas for interesting content for young people.
Organisation of different types of articles, presentation, style.

Range
Language for describing.
Language for analysing.
Language for hypothesising and recommending.

Appropriacy of register and format
Proposal format – may make use of clear section headings.
Register appropriate to semi-formal relationship.

Organisation and cohesion
Well-structured sections.
Clear presentation of ideas.
Clear linking and paragraphing.

Target reader
Would understand what the writer is proposing.

Question 3: *Protecting endangered animals, birds and plants*

Content
Description of why forms of nature and wild life are endangered, and concrete suggestions for helping to protect them.

Range
Language of description, analysis and suggestion.

Appropriacy of register and format
Register and format appropriate for a letter to a magazine. Register must be consistent.

Organisation and cohesion
Early reference to reason for writing. Clear organisation of points. Adequate use of linking and paragraphing.

Target reader
Readers would have a clear idea of the writer's suggestions for saving endangered species.

Question 4: 'Good Neighbours'

Content
Description of a difficult situation.
How the neighbour helped out.
Conclusions about what makes a good neighbour.

Range
Language of description and narration.

Appropriacy of register and format
Register appropriate for a popular magazine.
Article format could lend itself to headings.

Organisation and cohesion
Clear development of description and narration.
Adequate use of linking and paragraphing.

Target reader
Would be interested in reading the story of the event, understand why the neighbour was so appreciated by the writer and what, in the opinion of the writer, makes a good neighbour.

Question 5(a): The Accidental Tourist

Content
Clear reference to the book chosen.
Description and analysis of reasons for the failure of the marriage of Sarah and Macon. Evaluation of whether Macon's comment is true or not.

Range
Language of description, narration and evaluation.

Appropriacy of register and format
Neutral article.

Organisation and cohesion
Clear presentation and development of ideas. Appropriate linking and paragraphing. Clear conclusion.

Target reader
Would understand the viewpoint of the writer and have a clear idea of the reasons for the failure of the marriage of Sarah and Macon.

Question 5(b): The Day of the Triffids

Content
Clear reference to the book chosen.
Evaluation of whether the statement is true or not.
Description of what the triffids are and what they do, and reference to other characters and how they respond to the situation.

Range
Language of description, narration, comparison and evaluation.

Appropriacy of register and format
Formal letter appropriate for a literary magazine. Register must be consistent throughout.

Organisation and cohesion
Clear presentation and development of ideas with appropriate linking of paragraphs from the introduction to the main body of the letter. Clear conclusion.

Target reader
Would be clear about the writer's viewpoint on the matter.

Question 5(c): Our Man in Havana

Content
Close reference to the book chosen.
Description of the portrayal of Wormold as a secret agent, and an analysis of how far the novel is a typical spy story.

Range
Language of description, narration, analysis and evaluation.

Appropriacy of register and format
Review with register and format appropriate to the Arts Section of a newspaper. Register must be consistent throughout.

Organisation and cohesion
Clear presentation and development of ideas. Appropriate paragraphing and linking. Clear conclusion.

Target reader
Would be informed about the book and the portrayal of Wormold as a secret agent, and how far the novel is a typical spy story.

Paper 3   **Use of English** (1 hour 30 minutes)

Part 1   (one mark for each correct answer)

1 who   2 to   3 when   4 having   5 of   6 due / thanks / owing
7 what   8 its / the   9 no   10 it   11 into   12 only
13 whose   14 because / as / since   15 could / may / might

Part 2   (one mark for each correct answer)

16 infancy   17 institutions   18 exclusively   19 insight
20 disappearing   21 commitment   22 inaccessible   23 loneliness
24 immersion   25 undeniably

Part 3   (two marks for each correct answer)

26 reflection   27 bear   28 stage   29 line   30 volume   31 moved

Part 4   (one mark for each correct section)

32 were (completely) taken (1) + aback (completely) at / by (1)
33 given (1) + a standing ovation (1)
34 matter (1) + how late it (1)
35 no idea (of) what (1) + was going (1)
36 (many) hours (have passed) since OR (many) hours ago that (1) + I (first) joined (1)
37 any / a likelihood / possibility / chance (1) + of (my / me) having a (private / quiet) (1)
38 look / are (remarkably / very / incredibly) alike (1) + in the (1)
39 do / can we account for (1) + the fact that the / the way (that) the / why the (1)

Part 5   (questions 40–43 two marks for each correct answer)

40 They process the information according to their experience and needs.

41 By seeing them regularly many times.

42 (They're like a net) – they filter information / data from the outside world / they prevent certain things / information / data from passing through.

43 Instinctively but with cultural differences

44 (one mark for each content point, up to ten marks for summary skills)
The paragraph should include the following points:
  i   seeing parts rather than the whole – flecks of colour / notes
  ii not being able to distinguish objects
  iii too much noise to pick out sounds
  iv it would put our lives in danger

Paper 4   **Listening** (40 minutes approximately)

Part 1   (one mark for each correct answer)
1 B   **2** C   **3** B   **4** C   **5** C   **6** A   **7** C   **8** B

Part 2   (one mark for each correct answer)
9 rattle   **10** cliff faces/cliffs   **11** window(-)sills   **12** repopulate
13 cover   **14** nesting   **15** a/one hundred/100   **16** (deliberate) neglect/
being neglected (deliberately)   **17** locations

Part 3   (one mark for each correct answer)
18 B   **19** C   **20** A   **21** D   **22** D

Part 4   (one mark for each correct answer)
23 T   **24** B   **25** C   **26** C   **27** T   **28** T

Transcript   *Certificate of Proficiency in English Listening Test. Test 3.*

I'm going to give you the instructions for this test.

I'll introduce each part of the test and give you time to look at the questions.

At the start of each piece you'll hear this sound:

tone

You'll hear each piece twice.

Remember, while you're listening, write your answers on the question paper.

You'll have five minutes at the end of the test to copy your answers onto the separate answer sheet.

There will now be a pause. You must ask any questions now, because you must not speak during the test.

[pause]

Now open your question paper and look at Part One.

[pause]

PART 1   *You'll hear four different extracts. For questions 1 to 8, choose the answer (A, B or C) which fits best according to what you hear. There are two questions for each extract.*

Extract 1   [pause]

tone

Interviewer:	Reading your book about your career exploits, I have to say it does sound to me as if you've done what a lot of kids dream of, and managed to make a living out of, let's face it, larks, high spirits. It's akin to having the nerve to go to a company and ask for a million pounds to go on holiday.
Balloonist:	It's been wonderful.
Interviewer:	Long before this you started as a photographer.
Balloonist:	Yes, I've always liked imagery – that's part of the reason why I got involved in all these dreams, as you call them, of adventure. It's pure theatre, really.
Interviewer:	And you did a spell in advertising, I read.
Balloonist:	Yes, I did … and it was at that time in 1975 when I had my first balloon flight and in those days they really were the stuff of dreams, and it occurred to me that there must be a possibility to do something here with these huge billboards in the sky and to make a living out of it.

[pause]

tone

[The recording is repeated.]

[pause]

Extract 2   [pause]

tone

Presenter:	Robin Adams, you've recently published a book of photographs of famous women, with the proceeds going to a number of charities. How did you decide who to photograph? Are they people you had an interest in already because they're very high profile? Or did you think, there's a hook there? And I'm actually interested in photographing this person.

Robin Adams:	Well, although they are all, as you say, high-profile women, we went about this in a low-key way. I'd heard of most of them, or, at least, their reputations, and had seen their various media images. There's always more to people than meets the eye, or the camera lens – and it was that something I wanted to expose. But this proved more of a thorny issue than I'd expected.
Presenter:	Oh really, I thought it would have been easier, they would have known exactly how to present themselves. They've done it so many times before.
Robin Adams:	Well, in my work, I get behind the veneer of the face. The women feel secure enough to open up about themselves, and I have to be careful not to betray too much of that.

[pause]

tone

[The recording is repeated.]

[pause]

Extract 3

[pause]

tone

I'm ringing about Stoke City football team. I've been a supporter of theirs for years. You'll have noticed in Saturday's match just how much we miss Steve Harris. We lack the power up front since he's gone. There were some nice touches from Evans, but the real strength that Harris represented, that's served us well over the years, was just missing on Saturday. It was a gaping hole in Stoke's attack, and I'm sure the manager's regretting selling him. I mean, we don't need the £11 million that Barcelona paid us, we need our goal-scorer back! If you speak to the Stoke fans, most of them will say no amount of training will produce another Harris. He provided the punch and that just wasn't there on Saturday. No wonder we lost! Still, for a good thirty minutes our lads dominated the field. They showed some spirit, I must say. They haven't thrown in the towel yet, so provided we get a good replacement for Harris, (and the manager'd better get it right this time!) maybe there'll be light at the end of the tunnel after all.

[pause]

tone

[The recording is repeated.]

[pause]

Extract 4

[pause]

tone

When we managed to get it hoisted, for the first time since 1800, well, it was a struggle, but thank goodness, we did it. So then this immense amount of sail was hanging in the museum. I thought people would come in and go Wow! and then read the relevant information boards we'd put underneath. But there was a new dimension to this exhibition that I simply hadn't envisaged. People felt as if they were travelling back in time, because here they could see for themselves the reality of damage to a sailing ship on the high seas two centuries ago. You can see this great rent, which is about eight metres deep in the centre, and as you go closer to the cloth, not only do you get this sort of shine on the cloth itself, and you can see how it's aged and coloured, but at various points there are gunpowder stains of shots that must have passed through it, so again there's the reality. This isn't just a textbook or a computer game about history for you to look at, this is the…

[pause]

tone

[The recording is repeated.]

[pause]

That's the end of Part One.

Now turn to Part Two.

[pause]

PART 2   *You will hear a short talk about a bird of prey called the kestrel. For questions 9 to 17, complete the sentences with a word or short phrase.*

You now have forty-five seconds in which to look at Part Two.

[pause]

tone

Interviewer: Today we're very pleased to welcome Sean Pearce, from the British Nature Trust, who is going to talk about one of the most beautiful birds to be seen in Britain: the kestrel. Sean…

Sean Pearce: Thank you. I'm here to launch the Trust's publicity campaign. Recent, relatively small-scale research we've carried out is indicating a significant decline in kestrel numbers and basically we're asking the public to help us get our statistics even more accurate.

But first, let me give you a few facts on the bird to help in sighting and a little background information and an explanation of the cause of some of its problems. The kestrel – its unusual name comes from the old French for a rattle – and that refers not to the fluttering wing movement but to its cry. This is very distinctive. It has the capacity to hang in the air for long periods with its wings vibrating so rapidly you can hardly see the movement. This is a picture of a mature male hovering. Notice its beautiful plumage in different shades of brown and cream and its easily recognised fluted tail – the picture is reproduced for you in the survey material to help in identification.

Now, before the diversification of their habitat in the last hundred years or so, kestrels were solely to be found nesting on cliff faces and their main prey was the vole – a small mouse-like creature in the countryside but which now will be unfamiliar to many of you. But, *now*, kestrels are increasingly making their home in towns where they're not an uncommon sight these days, they settle on the window sills of houses, skyscrapers etc. Now, turning to food in this new habitat, they depend not on their rural staple of voles, who don't appear to do very well in this setting, but on whichever small rodents they can find, and these are to be

143

found in abundance. Kestrels have also found a viable habitat in upland areas, mainly the preserve of sheep farming, which is proving to be a problem, as we shall see.

Kestrels have actually been known to be highly successful in keeping up their numbers over the years because of their notable ability to quickly repopulate. How this works is simple – they aren't dependent on one locale and can gradually move to where the habitat is more favourable. But this is only effective when problems affect a small area. Difficulties at a macro level are now beginning to affect them. For example, upland kestrels suffer due to increasing sheep densities. Their grazing decreases the vegetation which provides cover for the main upland kestrel food, the vole, which of course, in turn means a large population of the birds of prey cannot be maintained. These problems have been compounded by long periods of heavy precipitation – mainly rain, but also snow, which causes nesting difficulties.

Now let's have a look at some of the population statistics. Excuse me, there are thought to be in the region of 50,000 breeding pairs – that's 100,000 adults – left in the UK, which means, with an average of three offspring per pair, circa 250,000 birds. But kestrels have a relatively low survival rate when young, which helps cushion extremes in population – a built-in control, if you like. Only a proportion survive – many succumbing in infancy because of their parents' deliberate neglect. Now, because of the changes mentioned earlier, the population is falling further and will soon, we believe, not be able to recover. Something *must* be done and that's where the public come in!

What we ask of you is to take two or three of these sighting forms, I'll pass some out in a moment, but I'll also leave a pile at the back, which you can fill in when you have a sighting. They ask for information about numbers, timing and, *crucially*, location. There is a picture, as promised, and simple diagrammatic information to help you establish whether what you have seen is really a kestrel and not confuse it with, for example, a peregrine falcon.

Thank you very much indeed for your time and attention. I hope you'll be able to help us.

[pause]

Now you'll hear Part Two again.

tone

[The recording is repeated.]

[pause]

That's the end of Part Two.

Now turn to Part Three.

[pause]

PART 3   *You will hear the historian, George Davies, talking about society and the theatre in England in the time of William Shakespeare. For questions 18 to 22, choose the answer (A, B, C or D) which fits best according to what you hear.*

You now have one minute in which to look at Part Three.

[pause]

tone

Interviewer: We welcome today Professor George Davies from the University of Wales. Professor Davies is an expert on society in sixteenth-century England, the time of Queen Elizabeth the First and, of course, Shakespeare. So how would you categorise society at that time, Professor?

Professor: Well, it was certainly a society undergoing dramatic changes in which there was an explosion of interest in the language, even though the printed word hadn't become universally available. We don't quite know exactly how many people could read and write but literacy would not have extended to all levels of society. Some historians call it an illiterate society, but that seems rather pejorative. No, the best way of putting it, in my view, is to refer to it as a *pre*-literate society, like most societies that have ever been on the planet. In fact our society, in which we tend to expect everybody to be literate, is the one which is out of step.

Interviewer: So how did this pre-literacy affect ability to communicate at that time?

Professor: What it meant was that the prime form of communication was direct speech, face to face, which means communication involving the body, the stance, the distance between people. It also meant that people were much more finely tuned to the spoken word, they could take in more of it, they could listen in a more acute way. It's therefore quite natural that the art form which corresponds to that particular situation should be drama.

Interviewer: One thing that has always puzzled me is where did the actors in the sixteenth century learn their craft? Were there any drama schools then?

Professor: Well, Shakespeare's actors, the boys and the older men in his company, didn't actually have any acting training before they joined his company. You see, in Shakespeare's day you learned your school work by repeating it out loud all day long. The arts of oratory and rhetoric were part of your normal education and they were also the means by which you learned. So they had wonderful voice training, which enabled them to develop an individual style.

Interviewer: I've always thought of the Elizabethan society as one that revelled in its voice, that at its heart delighted in giving voice to words. Would that be correct?

Professor: I would certainly think that the atmosphere in the average theatre of the time would surprise us today. I believe it would sound and feel more like a present day football ground! In a modern theatre there's a sort of reverential hush as the darkness descends and we feel, you know, that we're in some sort of temple devoted to the worship of great art. But then, the atmosphere would have been much noisier. Remember Shakespeare and his contemporaries had theatres which were open to the sky, and so the noise of the city, the shouts of the street sellers, the neighing of horses and so forth would add to and mix with the sounds of the stage and indeed, in my view, would comment on them.

Interviewer: So, in the same way, this was not a world for the shy or the softly spoken?

Professor: Not at all. People's voices in the sixteenth century, it seems to me, wouldn't have been geared to the exchange of intimate revelations about the self. This is a notion of speaking that is a twentieth-century concept, as is our notion that a play should give you the intimate, personal feelings of the author or of a character on the stage. Then, art was largely about external issues, how a country should be governed, how one should deal with rebellion, questions of that order.

Interviewer: Fascinating, Professor. I'd like at this point to bring in another speaker who is going to tell us about Elizabethan court life and how Shakespeare…

[pause]

Now you'll hear Part Three again.

tone

[The recording is repeated.]

[pause]

That's the end of Part Three.

Now turn to Part Four.

[pause]

PART 4   *You will hear a conversation in which Clare and Tom, who teach English to foreign students at the same language school, discuss Tom's first week at the school. For questions 23 to 28, decide whether the opinions are expressed by only one of the speakers, or whether the speakers agree. Write C for Clare, T for Tom, or B for both, where they agree.*

You now have thirty seconds in which to look at Part Four.

[pause]

tone

Clare: Hello, Tom. How are you finding teaching here?

Tom: Bit early to say, really, Clare. But I get the odd feeling that somehow the school's successful despite itself.

Clare: How do you mean?

Tom: Well, it *claims* to be really up-to-date, but the buildings and furniture have seen better days, and the equipment's on its last legs, yet amazingly the students seem happy.

Clare: Maybe the good atmosphere is partly *because* the building and things aren't up to much. People don't feel they always have to be on their best behaviour.

Tom: That just sounds like an excuse for being an also-ran! These days you can't compete unless you can really provide the best. That's the trouble with these small family-owned schools. So many of the owners still seem to be in the Dark Ages.

Clare: In what way?

Tom: They seem to believe that if the teaching's good enough, they'll get students, but quality doesn't sell itself these days, if it ever did.

Clare: That's because most of the students come through word of mouth. Though I don't know how long that'll keep the school going. So many other schools have really *good* marketing machines. But I suppose we're going to have to bite the bullet. I doubt if there'll be a place much longer for family-owned schools, the way things are going, with so many being taken over by large companies that own several schools.

Tom: Do you think there's a chance of surviving if they find a niche?

Clare: Like English for business, or for university, you mean?

Tom: Yes.

Clare: That's a point. There are some very successful ones that have stayed one-offs.

Tom: Well, their days are numbered if you ask me. More and more are being bought by companies.

Clare: Yes. Some companies seem to offer a whole range of subjects, not just English.

Tom: I think that's good, because they can bring together a mixture of teachers of different subjects.

Clare: That's all very well, but it doesn't do much for your professional development, does it?

Tom: Surely it gives a different perspective on the classroom? A geography teacher, say, might give you fresh ideas that you can apply in teaching English or maths.

Clare: I've always found it a real eye-opener talking to other English teachers. Because people's approaches to teaching the same subject can vary so much. I sometimes feel I'm not on the same wavelength as science teachers!

Tom: Oh Clare, honestly!

Clare: Well maybe I'm exaggerating a bit, but you know what I mean.

Tom: Actually I sometimes feel that about classes, you know? And I feel it's my role as the teacher to make sure we get on all right, but I can't always do it.

Clare: Surely it depends on the class too? Each class develops its own culture, and you may not be able to do anything about it. You just have to accept that you don't get on with every class.

Tom: I reckon that's a bit of a cop-out, really. I'm sure you ought to be flexible enough to deal with any class effectively, but I can't always do it.

Clare: Maybe it comes with experience. Do you think you'll stay here long?

Tom: Depends how it pans out. I need to believe I'm doing something worthwhile, even if the money isn't brilliant. I hope that comes, when I've had a chance to get settled.

Clare: It doesn't matter that much to me, I suppose, because I put a lot of energy into other things. So I could put up with quite a lot, as long as I've got enough to live on, of course.

Tom: Mm. I wish I had the time for other things. I'm sure...

[pause]

Now you'll hear Part Four again.

tone

[The recording is repeated.]

[pause]

That's the end of Part Four.

There will now be a pause of five minutes for you to copy your answers onto the separate answer sheet. Be sure to follow the numbering of all the questions. I'll remind you when there is one minute left, so that you're sure to finish in time.

[pause]

You have one more minute left.

[pause]

That's the end of the test. Please stop now. Your supervisor will now collect all the question papers and answer sheets.

Test 4 Key

Paper 1   **Reading** (1 hour 30 minutes)

Part 1   (one mark for each correct answer)

1 A	2 C	3 B	4 D	5 B	6 A	7 A	8 C	9 A
10 B	11 D	12 C	13 C	14 B	15 A	16 D		
17 C	18 D							

Part 2   (two marks for each correct answer)

19 C	20 D	21 B	22 A	23 B	24 A	25 C	26 A

Part 3   (two marks for each correct answer)

27 E	28 C	29 H	30 B	31 G	32 A	33 D

Part 4   (two marks for each correct answer)

34 B	35 B	36 D	37 B	38 C	39 C	40 A

Paper 2   **Writing** (2 hours)

Task-specific mark schemes

Question 1: Fast food restaurant

Content

Major points:

Discussion of: The advantages versus the drawbacks, e.g.
- encouraging more people to visit the town
- the possible increase in revenue
- the interest generated in local history

Range

Language for expressing and supporting views, and for making recommendations.

Appropriacy of register and format

Appropriate format for a proposal – may make use of headings.

Organisation and cohesion

Ideas organised and well-structured.
Adequate use of paragraphing and linking.

Target reader

The local council would understand the writer's viewpoint.

Question 2: Review of an adventure holiday

Content
Description of the adventure holiday, with reference to exploring interesting places, meeting different people and experiencing a different lifestyle, as well as some kind of recommendation, relevant to students wanting a cheap but exciting holiday.

Range
Language of description, narration, evaluation and recommendation.

Appropriacy of register and format
Formal/informal register appropriate for a review in a college magazine. Register must be consistent throughout.

Organisation and cohesion
Clear development of ideas with adequate use of linking and paragraphing, and possible use of headings.

Target reader
Would be informed about the holiday.
Would be able to decide whether or not it was a holiday they would want to experience.

Question 3: Improving education in your country

Content
Description of present provision of education, with an analysis and evaluation of areas that could be improved, followed by concrete suggestions for bringing about improvement.

Range
Language of description, analysis, suggestion and recommendation.

Appropriacy of register and format
Register and format appropriate for a proposal – may make use of section headings.
Register must be consistent throughout.

Organisation and cohesion
Clear organisation of content with adequate use of linking and paragraphing.

Target reader
The Minister would have a clear understanding of the ideas put forward.

Question 4: 'I've always wanted to learn how to...'

Content
Description of the particular skill the writer wants to acquire, plus an explanation of what is attractive about this skill. Description of what the writer would do with this skill.

Range
Language of description.

Appropriacy of register and format
Register and format appropriate for a magazine article. Possible use of section headings.

Organisation and cohesion
Ideas clearly organised. Adequate use of paragraphing and linking.

Target reader
Would have a clear idea of what skill the writer wanted to learn and what they would do with it.

Question 5(a): The Accidental Tourist

Content
Clear reference to the book chosen.
Recommendation of the book leading to emphasis on portrayal of Alexander and his relationship with his mother, Muriel, and with Macon.

Range
Language of description, narration and recommendation. Some language of description and narration relating to the characters in question and their relationships.

Appropriacy of register and format
Formal letter.

Organisation and cohesion
Clear presentation and development of ideas with appropriate linking of paragraphs from the introduction to the main body of the letter and the conclusion.

Target reader
Would know whether the novel would be suitable for the proposed exhibition.

Question 5(b): The Day of the Triffids

Content
Clear reference to the book chosen.
Description of the dramatic events in the story, and a description of the impact on the characters.

Range
Language of description and narration.

Appropriacy of register and format
Consistent and appropriate style for that of a report.

Organisation and cohesion
Clear presentation and development of ideas, with appropriate linking and paragraphing. May make use of section headings. Clear conclusion.

Target reader
Would be informed about the events and characters in the novel.

Question 5(c): Our Man in Havana

Content
Close reference to the book chosen.
Reference to how the relationship develops over the three visits Wormold makes to Dr Hasselbacher's flat.

Range
Language of description, narration and evaluation.

Appropriacy of register and format
Register appropriate to an article for a literary magazine.

Organisation and cohesion
Clear presentation and development of ideas. The account of the three visits can be dealt with together or separately. Appropriate linking and paragraphing required. Clear conclusion.

Target reader
Would have a clear idea of the characters of Wormold and Dr Hasselbacher, and how their relationship develops.

Paper 3   Use of English (1 hour 30 minutes)

Part 1   (one mark for each correct answer)

1 to   2 its   3 giving / considering   4 but / yet / (al)though   5 more
6 put   7 Despite   8 with   9 into   10 addition   11 should
12 as   13 not   14 one   15 far

Part 2   (one mark for each correct answer)

16 technological   17 anxieties   18 unquestionably   19 assumption
20 destructive   21 overwhelmingly   22 beings   23 pessimistically
24 imperfections   25 heights

Part 3   (two marks for each correct answer)

26 cleared   27 state   28 set   29 remain   30 claimed   31 fall

Part 4   (one mark for each correct section)

32 being driven by Paul's son (1) + at the time (1)
33 it not been for Nick's advice (1) + I would / I'd (1)
34 no point / time / stage (1) + did the police (actually) (ever) accuse (1)
35 much / a lot / a great deal to choose (1) + between (either of) (1)
36 is a total ban (1) + on (you / your) smoking (1)
37 makes (1) + no difference to Jenny (1)
38 improvement (1) + in the way the football team played / performed (1)
39 singled out the school library (1) + for criticism (1)

Part 5   (questions 40–43 two marks for each correct answer)

40 doom-mongers
41 the way in which old jobs are replaced by a greater number of new jobs
     because of changes in technology
42 innovations
43 Bill seems to be very interested in new technologies, so it's a surprise to find he
     uses something which is so old-fashioned
44 (one mark for each content point, up to ten marks for summary skills)
     The paragraph should include the following points:
     i   technology doesn't necessarily lead to unemployment
     ii technology doesn't lead to low incomes
     iii new technologies don't completely replace old ones
     iv people sometimes prefer to keep old technologies

Paper 4   Listening (40 minutes approximately)

Part 1   (one mark for each correct answer)
1 C   2 B   3 B   4 A   5 C   6 A   7 B   8 A

Part 2   (one mark for each correct answer)
9 field training   10 tent   11 volcano (called Mount Erebus)
12 (flat (and) white) plain   13 roof (made out of lots of snow)
14 laboratories   15 month's salary   16 clothing / clothes (on display)
17 heroic failures

Part 3   (one mark for each correct answer)
18 B   19 A   20 D   21 C   22 C

Part 4   (one mark for each correct answer)
23 B   24 B   25 M   26 M   27 B   28 F

Transcript   *Certificate of Proficiency in English Listening Test. Test 4.*

I'm going to give you the instructions for this test.

*I'll introduce each part of the test and give you time to look at the
questions.*

At the start of each piece you'll hear this sound:

tone

You'll hear each piece twice.

*Remember, while you're listening, write your answers on the question
paper.*

You'll have five minutes at the end of the test to copy your answers onto the separate answer sheet.

There will now be a pause. You must ask any questions now, because you must not speak during the test.

[pause]

Now open your question paper and look at Part One.

[pause]

PART 1   *You'll hear four different extracts. For questions 1 to 8, choose the answer (A, B or C) which fits best according to what you hear. There are two questions for each extract.*

Extract 1   [pause]

tone

And now to American composer Carl Ruggles, who is still, years after his death, a total enigma. He worked at an incredibly slow pace, discarded far more than he kept, and has left us barely enough works to fill two CDs. Ruggles by name and rugged by nature, he was truly a man of the great outdoors. And he was never one to mince his words when commenting on his fellow musicians. He said of the French composer Debussy, 'There's nothing wrong with him that two weeks in the open air wouldn't cure!' and of the great romantic German composer Brahms, 'Why does he always hide behind all those musical devices? Why doesn't he come out and show us he's a man?' Here now is an orchestral piece of his, called 'Men and Angels.' It has a chequered history, as Ruggles originally wrote it in 1920 and then destroyed parts of it, so it was later revised. It is played here by members of the…

[pause]

tone

[The recording is repeated.]

[pause]

Extract 2   [pause]

tone

… it's a French novel, a worthy first novel, and I was fascinated with this because it's about the friendship between two women, something which isn't often written about, and also two very different women. The narrator is in her thirties with two children, and she writes for a living and needs a babysitter. The girl she winds up with, who comes to her through various friends, could not be more different. So it's a novel about differences; the girl, who is seen to be feckless and lacking in any sense of duty, and the narrator, who is bound up in her work to the exclusion of virtually everything else. Although that leads you to the question of the nature, I mean, what *is* work?

The themes I really enjoyed but, unfortunately, I don't think the translation works – I can't get any sense of the women's social context – I felt they were locked in a beautiful white cube somewhere and that, if only I understood where they were, I might have a better handle on them. I feel the translator was too concerned with putting his own stamp on the work.

[pause]

tone

[The recording is repeated.]

[pause]

Extract 3   [pause]

tone

Sociologically speaking, bags are an interesting feature of modern society. How we carry them is important. They're carried in the hand, on the crook of the arm, over the shoulder, on the back, in the form of pockets. Bags in fact are a way of keeping and displaying connections between our front and other parts of us, less visible, more vulnerable. A recent trend on the High Street was for girls to wear exquisitely functionless little rucksacks in the middle of their backs.

We often carry our cash, credit cards and other valuables in bags of one form or another, so they *can* show wealth and buying power. However, they also symbolise poverty and redundancy. The expression 'to give someone the sack' probably dates from 17th century France. In those days workmen provided their own tools and carried them in a bag, *sac* in French, which they took away with them upon leaving. So the word *sack* evolved from referring to the container for the workman's prized possessions, to the associated action of leaving a job, with the emphasis on *unwilling* departure.

[pause]

tone

[The recording is repeated.]

[pause]

Extract 4   [pause]

tone

Woman: You know I don't really enjoy going to the cinema anymore. I mean they spend millions now on making films and for what?

Man: Mmm, that level of expenditure seems to pay dividends. Cinema audiences have changed, and it looks to me as if most films just try to appeal to mass audiences.

Woman: Yes, they seem to make them to a format.

Man: It's 'oh, a disaster to overcome and then all live happily ever after'. Anything remotely sophisticated never makes it to the screen.

Woman: Well, they say cinema audiences have changed and it looks to me as if they're just trying to appeal to the lowest common denominator. Mind you, you still get a good cross-section going.

Man: The ones I do enjoy are based on true-life stories. At least you feel you're seeing something real.

Woman: Hmm… I'm not sure about that. They always twist the facts to make it more exciting I suppose.

Man: Yeah, but I bet they do it because otherwise anybody in the story who is still around could see themselves really badly set up on screen – and would probably take them to court. *(laughs)*

Woman: Yes… Anyway, real life is just much more mundane, isn't it?

Man: Well, I don't think anyone would pay to see a film of my life.

[pause]

tone

[The recording is repeated.]

[pause]

That's the end of Part One.

Now turn to Part Two.

[pause]

PART 2 *You will hear a scientist talking about his first visit to the Antarctic. For questions 9 to 17, complete the sentences with a word or short phrase.*

You now have forty-five seconds in which to look at Part Two.

[pause]

tone

Presenter: Dozens of scientists travel to the Antarctic every year to gather information on a range of subjects. Richard Hollingham is one of those scientists and he's here today to tell us about his first trip south and the survival course he and all other scientists have to go through when they arrive in the Antarctic.

Richard: Well, the first day was spent getting accustomed to the sub-zero temperatures, which meant sliding down a glacier on our bottoms followed by a night sleeping out on the snow. This is what they call field training and anyone who has to spend significant periods of time working away from the main bases has to do it. And I really needed this training because on that first trip I was heading to an area of sea ice, where I would have to spend three months, in a tent! Can you imagine? This was going to be quite an experience.

Anyway, the setting for our first day's training was in the shadow of Mount Erebus, a volcano on the edge of the Ross Ice shelf. When I was there, a few wisps of sulphurous smoke rose from the summit of the crater. Behind us was a glacier and ahead a flat white plain which went all the way to the South Pole. The first day's training culminated in the construction of snow shelters. We were lucky with the weather. It was around minus ten and bright sun. There were twelve of us on this course and we split into teams and each team opted for a different type of shelter. The Canadians chose the igloo type, the New Zealanders the 'dig through a pile of snow' option and we went for a trench. We foolishly thought it would be the easiest. So we set to work and after a couple of hours, it was beautiful, it was deep and long but unfortunately far too wide. Everyone else had resounding success with their efforts but we were miserable failures. The idea was that what we'd dug should then be able to take a roof, but no matter how hard we tried, we couldn't get enough snow in blocks to bridge the gap. So in the end all we had was a long hole and that's how we came to sleep outside at night in one of the coldest places in the world.

This wasn't exactly the start we'd hoped for and we wistfully remembered what we'd seen of base camp at McMurdoch Sound; it was more like a town. Of course, there are the laboratories, but it's even got cable television. Society on base is fascinating. There's a black market in what at first seem very unlikely things. Things like newspapers and mineral water can change hands for considerable amounts of money; there's a rumour that salad greens, the most sought-after thing which are only occasionally shipped in, can fetch up to a month's salary for a dinner's worth.

The whole area around the base camp is full of reminders of some of the earliest explorers to that region; people like the British explorers, Shackleton and Scott. In fact, a few miles up the coast, the hut which Shackleton and Scott stayed in has still got the clothing they wore on display. Further on again, there's a base called the Scott Base and it's full of photographs of him, you know he lost his life on the return journey from the South Pole. The odd thing is there are no pictures of the man who actually got to the South Pole first, a Norwegian called Amundsen. I put this to a Norwegian on our survival course and he said Amundsen made it all look so easy whereas Scott had made it look much harder, the stuff of legends. So we carried on that British tradition of making things seem hard. Our training officer labelled us the 'heroic failures' because he'd never seen anybody get a shelter so wrong despite putting so much effort into it.

[pause]

Now you'll hear Part Two again.

tone

[The recording is repeated.]

[pause]

That's the end of Part Two.

Now turn to Part Three.

[pause]

PART 3   *You will hear part of a radio interview with a social worker. For questions 18 to 22, choose the answer (A, B, C or D) which fits best according to what you hear.*

You now have one minute in which to look at Part Three.

[pause]

tone

Presenter:	In 1980 Tim Jarman left a comfortable university post for the insalubrious Northdown council estate, where housing is provided for the unemployed and those with low incomes. Here he set up a project to provide youth amenities. Tim, why did you give up your position at a university for a job on an estate?
Tim Jarman:	Well, I was writing a book about social policy at the time, and I felt a bit of a hypocrite writing about poverty, telling people who work with the underprivileged what to do and not doing it myself. So I managed to get a grant from a charity, who helped me set up the Northdown Project.
Presenter:	When you got there, you moved into a house, an old doctor's surgery?
Tim Jarman:	Yes. I didn't really know what I was going to do, except that I was going to be rooted in the community. I was fortunate in making a friendship with a local teenager. We just knocked on doors, and said, 'What do *you* think we should do?' Most people said, 'Do something about the kids in the street.' The kids in the street were saying, 'It's boring, we need things to do,' and out of that came very extensive youth clubs, which for the first few years, in fact, met in my house.
Presenter:	What did the youngsters do there?
Tim Jarman:	Very ordinary things. You know, table-tennis, snooker, ball games. It was very crowded in my house, of course, and later on we found somewhere larger. But I think the essence was that it was their place. And there was an old greenhouse, just a lean-to against our house, and about 15 teenagers took that over as their den. And they came every night and met up with their friends there. So they were kept out of trouble, but they weren't having adults breathing down their neck. That's what counted, I think.
Presenter:	After 10 years there, you moved away, but you went back to Northdown later, didn't you, to see how these teenagers had got on? What'd happened to them?
Tim Jarman:	Well, I'd found a way of measuring the likelihood of their getting into trouble. When they first came to us, most of them were brought up in difficult circumstances, had problems at school, were in trouble with the police and so on. I set up a kind of risk table and worked out that 39% were at high risk of future unemployment, crime and unstable relationships. But the encouraging feature is that, now in their 30s, the majority of the youngsters have kept out of trouble, are in work and enjoy stable relationships. So the prediction was wrong, because something intervened to set things right. I'm not claiming our project was the whole factor, because clearly the availability of jobs, finding the right partner, making a good relationship were important, but all the 50 youngsters we interviewed said the project played a major part in their lives.
Presenter:	So, is there a formula you think could be applied elsewhere?
Tim Jarman:	Yes, the long-term nature of it, the combination of youth clubs and having social workers resident in the area who really get to know the young people. That's the core of it. The trouble is, our kind of project's no longer in the mainstream. Modern projects are very different, because the authorities are much keener on swift intervention, on targeting youngsters with problems, not treating them on a neighbourhood basis, a quick fix, in other words.
Presenter:	I know you're critical of the initiatives some governments are adopting, giving people advice and counselling on how to be good parents.

[pause]

Now you'll hear Part Three again.

tone

[The recording is repeated.]

[pause]

That's the end of Part Three.

Now turn to Part Four.

[pause]

PART 4   *You will hear part of a conversation in which two neighbours, Mary and Frank, are discussing current developments in museums. For questions 23 to 28, decide whether the opinions are expressed by only one of the speakers, or whether the speakers agree. Write M for Mary, F for Frank, or B for both, where they agree.*

You now have thirty seconds in which to look at Part Four.

[pause]

tone

Mary: How was your weekend, Frank? Do anything nice?

Frank: Yes Mary, I did actually. We all went to the Science Museum.

Mary: I shouldn't think your children were very pleased at being taken round a lot of dusty exhibits.

Frank: Well, I know that's what people think, but lots of museums are really interesting these days.

Mary: Well, if you say so.

Frank: I know why you're sceptical. I remember when museums used to be just row after row of glass cabinets full of rocks or dead insects…

Mary: Aren't they still?

Frank: They're more interactive now. Kids can press buttons and touch things. It's really child-friendly.

Mary: But I thought museums were for learning.

Frank: Education doesn't have to be dull or stuffy, does it?

Mary: Not nowadays, at any rate. But why did you choose the Science Museum? Your children aren't very keen on science, are they?

Frank: Well, that's the point. I wanted to give them some encouragement, sort of sugar the pill. Actually, I found them a good booklet on the museum in the local library first and so they got interested in the exhibits before we went.

Mary: That must have been helpful.

Frank: Mmm, and it saves time when you actually visit, if you know what to focus on.

Mary: What about the cost? Museums charge quite a lot now, don't they? They were all free years ago, when I took my children.

Frank: Well, that's all a bit up in the air at the moment. Some places are still free, some just charge £1 for adults, and some charge quite a hefty sum.

Mary: I can see that charging is a thorny issue. But the collections in museums are national assets. So everyone should be able to have equal access to them, shouldn't they?

Frank: There are *other* implications, like the theory that people are more likely to value something if they have to pay for it.

Mary: Um, but let's look at public libraries. They're a national resource too.

Frank: So?

Mary: Well, it would be quite wrong if the local authorities started charging for access to them, claiming it would make children appreciate books more.

Frank: But museums have to put on special events to attract more people, but books in a library don't change that much. And you know, some museums have an outreach system now, which I think is quite a positive move.

Mary: Does that mean they take dinosaur skeletons and paintings round the country in a van!

Frank: It would need a very large van for a dinosaur! No they send some of their collection, paintings etc. out to schools, libraries, community centres on temporary loan.

Mary: Oh, I see. Well, it *is* a long way to the big museums from little towns like this. Hmm, I suppose that's quite a creative use of resources.

Frank: Indeed.

Mary: What was the building itself like? I saw a programme on TV about a new museum in the North, and the architecture was lovely, very light and airy.

Frank: And I'm sure the sort of building really influences how you experience the contents.

Mary: Well, perhaps I'd better see the Science Museum for myself.

[pause]

Now you'll hear Part Four again.

tone

[The recording is repeated.]

[pause]

That's the end of Part Four.

There will now be a pause of five minutes for you to copy your answers onto the separate answer sheet. Be sure to follow the numbering of all the questions. I'll remind you when there is one minute left, so that you're sure to finish in time.

[pause]

You have one more minute left.

[pause]

That's the end of the test. Please stop now. Your supervisor will now collect all the question papers and answer sheets.

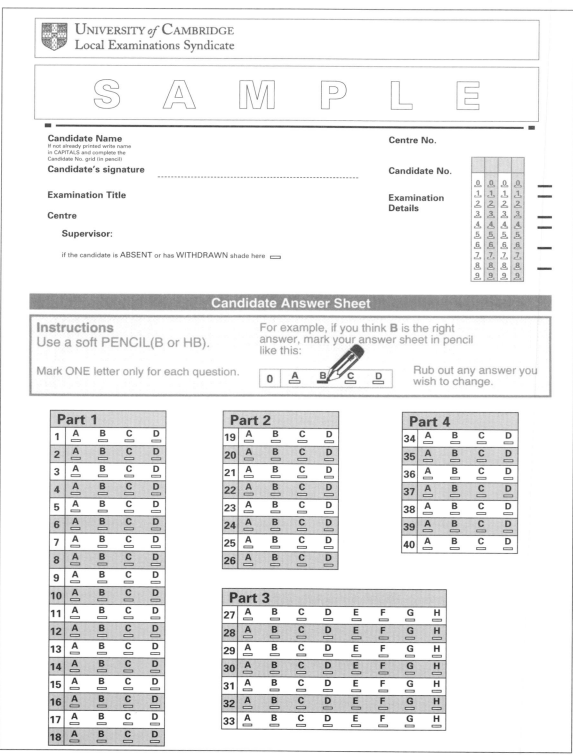

UNIVERSITY *of* CAMBRIDGE
Local Examinations Syndicate

S A M P L E

Candidate Name
If not already printed write name
in CAPITALS and complete the
Candidate No. grid (in pencil)

Candidate's signature

Examination Title

Centre

Supervisor:

if the candidate is ABSENT or has WITHDRAWN shade here

Centre No.

Candidate No.

**Examination
Details**

0	0	0	0
1	1	1	1
2	2	2	2
3	3	3	3
4	4	4	4
5	5	5	5
6	6	6	6
7	7	7	7
8	8	8	8
9	9	9	9

Answer Sheet 1

Part 1

Instructions

Use a soft PENCIL
(B or HB).

Rub out any answer
you wish to change,
with an eraser.

For **Parts 1, 2** and **3:**
Write your answer
clearly in CAPITAL
LETTERS.
Write one letter in each
box.

For example:

0 | M | A | Y | |

Answer **Parts 4** and **5**
on the second answer
sheet.

Write your answer
neatly in the spaces
provided.

You do not have to
write in capital letters for
Parts 4 and 5.

1   1 1 0
2   1 2 0
3   1 3 0
4   1 4 0
5   1 5 0
6   1 6 0
7   1 7 0
8   1 8 0
9   1 9 0
10   1 10 0
11   1 11 0
12   1 12 0
13   1 13 0
14   1 14 0
15   1 15 0

Part 2

16		1 16 0
17		1 17 0
18		1 18 0
19		1 19 0
20		1 20 0
21		1 21 0
22		1 22 0
23		1 23 0
24		1 24 0
25		1 25 0

Part 3

26		1 26 0
27		1 27 0
28		1 28 0
29		1 29 0
30		1 30 0
31		1 31 0

Continue with Parts 4 and 5 on Answer Sheet 2 ▶

UNIVERSITY *of* CAMBRIDGE
Local Examinations Syndicate

S A M P L E

Candidate Name
If not already printed write name
in CAPITALS and complete the
Candidate No. grid (in pencil)

Candidate's signature

Examination Title

Centre

Supervisor:

if the candidate is ABSENT or has WITHDRAWN shade here

Centre No.

Candidate No.

Examination Details

0	0	0	0
1	1	1	1
2	2	2	2
3	3	3	3
4	4	4	4
5	5	5	5
6	6	6	6
7	7	7	7
8	8	8	8
9	9	9	9

Answer sheet 2

Part 4

		32
32		0 1 2
33		33 0 1 2
34		34 0 1 2
35		35 0 1 2
36		36 0 1 2
37		37 0 1 2
38		38 0 1 2
39		39 0 1 2

163

Part 5

40		40 0 1 2
41		41 0 1 2
42		42 0 1 2
43		43 0 1 2

Part 5: question 44

For Examiner use only

Marks

Examiner number:
Team and Position

Content	0	1	2	3	4

Language	0	1.1	1.2	2.1	2.2	3.1	3.2	4.1	4.2	5.1	5.2

0 0 0 0
1 1 1 1
2 2 2 2
3 3 3 3
4 4 4 4
5 5 5 5
6 6 6 6
7 7 7 7
8 8 8 8
9 9 9 9

UNIVERSITY *of* CAMBRIDGE
Local Examinations Syndicate

S A M P L E

Candidate Name
If not already printed write name
in CAPITALS and complete the
Candidate No. grid (in pencil)

Candidate's signature

Examination Title

Centre

Supervisor:

if the candidate is ABSENT or has WITHDRAWN shade here ⊂⊃

Centre No.

Candidate No.

Examination Details

0	0	0	0
1	1	1	1
2	2	2	2
3	3	3	3
4	4	4	4
5	5	5	5
6	6	6	6
7	7	7	7
8	8	8	8
9	9	9	9

Candidate Answer Sheet

Mark test version (in PENCIL) A B C   Special arrangements   H

Instructions
Use a soft PENCIL (B or HB).
Rub out any answer you wish to change with an eraser.

For **Parts 1 and 3:**
Mark ONE letter only for each question.
For example, if you think B is the right answer,
mark your answer sheet like this:

0   A   B   C

For **Part 2:**
Write your answer clearly in
the space like this:

0   example

For **Part 4:**
Write ONE letter only, like this: 0   A

Part 1			
1	A	B	C
2	A	B	C
3	A	B	C
4	A	B	C
5	A	B	C
6	A	B	C
7	A	B	C
8	A	B	C

Part 2	Do not write here
9	1 9 0
10	1 10 0
11	1 11 0
12	1 12 0
13	1 13 0
14	1 14 0
15	1 15 0
16	1 16 0
17	1 17 0

Part 3				
18	A	B	C	D
19	A	B	C	D
20	A	B	C	D
21	A	B	C	D
22	A	B	C	D

Part 4	Do not write here
23	1 23 0
24	1 24 0
25	1 25 0
26	1 26 0
27	1 27 0
28	1 28 0